GRE
VOCABULARY
· ·
FLASH REVIEW

NEW YORK

Library of Congress Cataloging-in-Publication Data
GRE Vocabulary flash review. — 1st ed.
     p. ; cm.
  ISBN- 978-1-57685-781-6
  1. Vocabulary—Problems, exercises, etc. 2. Graduate Record Examination. I. LearningExpress (Organization)
  PE1449.G656 2011
  428.1—dc22

                                        2010053646

  Printed in the United States of America
9 8 7 6 5 4 3
First Edition

For more information or to place an order, contact LearningExpress at:
          2 Rector Street
          26th Floor
          New York, NY 10006

Or visit us at:
          www.learnatest.com

CONTENTS

INTRODUCTION

The GRE general test is designed to test applicants who are applying to graduate school. *GRE Vocabulary Flash Review* includes pronunciation guides, definitions, sample sentences, and synonyms for 600 of the words that most commonly appear on the Graduate Record Examination (GRE) general test. Studying and learning these words will help you succeed on the Verbal Reasoning sections of the exam.

About the GRE General Test

Beginning in August 2011, the Educational Testing Service (ETS) is offering a revised version of the GRE general test. The following information reflects the format of the revised general test; changes from the previous version of the test are also noted.

Beginning in August 2011, the GRE will include six sections. (The previous version included fewer but longer sections.)

It includes:

- An **Analytic Writing** section, for which you will write two short essays.
- Two **Verbal Reasoning** sections, which test reading comprehension.
- Two **Quantitative Reasoning** sections, which test mathematical concepts and skills.
- An unidentified **experimental section**.

Altogether, the test takes about three and a half hours to complete. The Analytic Writing section is always administered first; the other sections may follow in any order. In addition, a research section may conclude the test. As with the experimental section, your answers on this section will not count toward your final score.

Go to the ETS website for detailed information about each of these exam sections:

www.ets.org/gre

The Experimental Section

The experimental section may be a third Verbal Reasoning section, or it may be a third Quantitative Reasoning section. Because this section is experimental, and only designed to test questions for use on future exams, your answers on it will not count toward your final score. However, you will not know which section is the experimental section, so be sure to do your best on all parts of the exam.

Computer-Based Testing

All GRE general tests within the United States are administered by computer. (Only if you take the exam outside the United States, in an area where computer-based testing is unavailable, will you take a paper-based exam; these are administered a limited number of times each year.) Beginning in August 2011, the format of the computer-based exam will allow you to change answers within a section or skip questions and go back to them later—actions that were not permitted on the previous version of the computer-based exam. Although scratch paper is permitted, the exam is administered entirely by computer.

Vocabulary on the GRE General Test

Unlike the previous version of the GRE general test, the revised version does not include antonyms or analogies—question types that test the understanding of vocabulary out of context. This is good news for you! The context provided by a sentence or passage on which each question is based will help you determine the meaning of the words you study in this book and elsewhere.

Beginning in August 2011, the Verbal Reasoning sections of the GRE general test include the following three question types.

Reading Comprehension questions test your understanding of a text. The GRE general test includes about 10 Reading Comprehension passages, ranging in length from one paragraph to several; as few as one and as many as six questions may be asked about a given passage. These will comprise about half of the questions you will see on the Verbal Reasoning sections.

There are three kinds of Reading Comprehension questions:

- Some questions are traditional multiple-choice questions, in which you select one correct answer from among five choices.
- Some questions require you to select one, two, or three correct answers from among three choices. You cannot receive partial credit for your responses to these questions; you receive credit for your response only if you select all of the correct answers and nothing else.
- Some questions, require you to click on the sentence within the passage that meets a particular description.

Some Reading Comprehension questions will ask directly about the meaning of words within a passage. However, because the strength of your vocabulary is a crucial factor in your ability to understand what you read, vocabulary study should help you prepare for Reading Comprehension questions.

For **Text Completion** questions, you are presented with a brief passage, from which some words have been omitted. Your task is to select the words and/or phrases that complete the passage in a way that makes sense. If the passage includes just one blank, you will be offered five choices, only one of which fills in the blank correctly. If the passage includes two or three blanks, you will be offered three choices for each blank.

For **Sentence Equivalence** questions, you are presented with a single sentence that includes a blank. Your task is to select two words from among the choices provided, either of which could complete the sentence in a way that makes sense. The two completed sentences will be equivalent in meaning. You cannot receive partial credit for your responses to these questions; you receive credit for your response only if you select *both* correct answers.

Because of their more focused format, success with Text Completion and Sentence Equivalence questions depends greatly on the strength of your vocabulary.

ABOUT THIS BOOK

The 600 words in this book are presented in alphabetical order. Each page includes three words: On one side, the words are provided along with a guide to their pronunciation. On the reverse side, definitions, sample sentences, and synonyms are provided for each word. The pages are designed in this way so that you can quiz yourself on the meaning of each word.

The pronunciation of each word is given. Capital letters indicate stressed syllables, and the following spellings are used to represent some common sounds.

g	girl
j	jelly
k	kite, cat
s	sun, celery
z	zest, cheese
zh	measure

a	h<u>a</u>t
e	b<u>e</u>d
i	w<u>i</u>sh
o	m<u>o</u>p
u	c<u>u</u>p
ey	c<u>a</u>ke
ee	<u>ea</u>t
ahy	b<u>i</u>ke
oh	c<u>oa</u>t
yoo	m<u>u</u>sic
uh	<u>a</u>larm [schwa]
aw	r<u>a</u>w
ou	m<u>ou</u>se
oo	r<u>oo</u>m

The definitions provided for the words are not comprehensive, but rather focus your attention on the meanings that are the most common—and the most commonly tested. Synonyms are provided to further clarify the meaning of each word. Because the best way to learn vocabulary is to learn it in context, a sample sentence is provided for each word, to illustrate its use.

A word about spelling: yes, it does count! Take care to note and learn the distinction between such commonly confused words as *complacent* and *complaisant* and *discreet* and *discrete*. Also note the spelling of such words as *complement* (as opposed to *compliment*) and *imminent* (as opposed to *eminent*).

Using This Book for Vocabulary Study

In truth, vocabulary acquisition is the work of a lifetime. Don't try to learn all 600 words in this book at once. The best approach is to study the words in sets of about 12 or 15 words (4 or 5 pages) each day. The following is a suggested program of study:

- Review a set of words in the morning. Say each word aloud. Try to think of your own sentences using the words.
- Write the words down on a sheet of paper, and keep the sheet with you, checking it throughout the day to familiarize yourself with the list.
- In the evening, quiz yourself on the meaning of the words. Use a pencil to write a check next to the words you define correctly; review the words you are unable to define, along with the words you will study the next day.
- Periodically quiz yourself on the words you have already studied, to check that you have learned them.

A Last Word on Vocabulary Study: Read, Read, Read

Vocabulary is learned best when it is learned in context—that's why we've provided a sample sentence for each word in this book. The more frequently you encounter words in a variety of contexts, the better you will be able to remember them, and even discern the nuances of their meaning. So, the best way to learn GRE vocabulary is to read, read, read!

If you are currently an undergraduate, you're probably scrambling to keep up with your weekly reading assignments. As you read, pay attention to the vocabulary in each assignment. Take the time to note and look up the meaning of words you don't know. If you come across one of the words in this book, note the context in which it is used. You might even want to jot down the sentence on the page with the word in this book.

If you are not currently in school, the type of reading that will best prepare you for the GRE general test is nonfiction. Read the newspaper. Read serious magazines, such as *New Yorker*, *The Economist,* or *The Nation*. Read biographies. Choose a subject that matters to you, and read everything you can find on the topic. As you read, pay attention to the vocabulary you encounter; learn the words that are new to you, and note the use of words you have learned from this book.

GRE VOCABULARY

FLASH REVIEW

ABATE
(ah-BEYT)

. . . .

ABDICATE
(AB-di-keyt)

. . . .

ABERRANT
(ah-BER-uhnt)

A

to make or become less in degree, intensity, value, or amount

We waited for the storm to **abate** before we headed out.

Synonyms: decrease, diminish, reduce, subside

. . . .

to give up a right or responsibility, especially formally

Elizabeth II of England would probably not have become queen if her uncle, King Edward VIII, had not **abdicated**.

Synonyms: relinquish, renounce, resign

. . . .

going off the usual, normal, or right way; deviating from the usual or normal type

The **aberrant** weather during that rainy summer left many feeling as though there had not been any summer at all.

Synonyms: abnormal, atypical, deviant, unusual

ABEYANCE
(uh-BEY-uhns)

. . . .

ABJECT
(AB-jekt)

. . . .

ABJURE
(ab-JOOR)

A

a temporary state of inactivity

*We kept our travel plans in **abeyance** and did not go until we were certain that we had enough money for the trip.*

Synonyms: inactivity, recess, suspension

. . . .

completely hopeless

*They lost everything when their house burned down and have since lived in **abject** conditions, often homeless.*

Synonyms: downtrodden, miserable, wretched

. . . .

to formally reject, often under oath

*Though she had completely changed her ways, she could not **abjure** her former friends.*

Synonyms: forswear, renounce

ABSCOND
(ab-SKOND)

. . . .

ABSTEMIOUS
(ab-STEE-mee-uhs)

. . . .

ABYSMAL
(uh-BIZ-muhl)

A

to leave secretly and suddenly

*One minute the children were underfoot; the next minute, they **absconded** with all the cookies.*

Synonyms: disappear, escape, vanish

. . . .

restrained, especially with food and alcohol

*Since she began to do yoga, she has also been **abstemious** with both alcohol and junk food.*

Synonyms: frugal, moderate, restrained, temperate

. . . .

like an abyss: immeasurably great or low; hopelessly bad

*He wrote the term paper all in one night, and the results were **abysmal**.*

Synonyms: bottomless, vast, wretched

ACCOLADE
(A-kuh-LEYD)

· ·

ACERBIC
(uh-SUHR-bik)

· ·

ACCRUE
(uh-KROO)

A

an award or other expression of honor or praise

*Given the number of **accolades** she has received for her work on stage and in film, it is surprising just how humble she is.*

Synonyms: award, honor

. . . .

sour or harsh in taste, mood, or temperament

*He tried to hide his bad mood, but his **acerbic** reply gave his anger away.*

Synonyms: acidic, caustic, harsh, sharp

. . . .

to grow through additions

*As the years **accrue**, so does wisdom.*

Synonyms: accumulate, collect, increase

ACUMEN
(A-kyuh-muhn)

. . . .

ADAMANT
(A-duh-muhnt)

. . . .

ADMONISH
(ad-MO-nish)

insight or shrewdness, especially in practical matters

*Due to the combination of her personal warmth and business **acumen**, her new company was an instant success.*

Synonyms: discernment, insight, judgment, perception

. . . .

insistent, immovable

*Though the child protested, his parents were **adamant**: he had to be in bed by eight o'clock.*

Synonyms: determined, inflexible, resolute, stubborn, unyielding

. . . .

to advise against something; to gently scold or warn

*The teacher **admonished** the children for tracking mud down the hallways of the school.*

Synonyms: advise, reprimand, warn

ADULATION
(a-juh-LEY-shun)

. . . .

ADULTERATE
(uh-DUHL-tuh-REYT)

. . . .

AESTHETIC
(es-THE-tik)

A

excessive admiration, praise, or devotion; flattery

*The football star enjoyed the **adulation** of thousands of fans until it was revealed that he had cheated.*

Synonyms: devotion, fawning, flattery, worship

. . . .

to make impure by adding foreign or inferior elements, materials, or ingredients

*Do not **adulterate** this cake batter by using flour of such poor quality!*

Synonyms: cheapen, corrupt, dilute, weaken

. . . .

having to do with beauty or the arts

*Though the morality of the movie is question-able, its **aesthetic** qualities are admirable: it was beautifully filmed.*

Synonym: artistic

AFFINITY
(uh-FI-ni-tee)

. . . .

AGGRANDIZE
(uh-GRAN-dahyz)

. . . .

AGGREGATE
(A-gre-guht or A-gre-GEYT)

an attraction, especially one based on a similarity in interests

Countless young women have read and reread Jane Eyre, feeling an **affinity** *for its fierce heroine.*

Synonyms: affection, fondness, sympathy

. . . .

to make greater in size, power, or honor; to enhance the appearance of greatness

The dictator **aggrandized** *his power by taking control of the press and all other media.*

Synonyms: glorify, hype, inflate, strengthen

. . . .

(*adj.*) formed by grouping elements into one larger body

The **aggregate** *power of the teammates was far greater than you might imagine based on their individual talents.*

Synonyms: accumulated, collective

(*v.*) to group elements into one larger body

We need to **aggregate** *the survey results in order to have a clear picture of the overall data.*

Synonyms: assemble, collect, combine

(*n.*) a body of associated elements

In the **aggregate**, *her small daily efforts resulted in a gorgeous book of poems.*

Synonyms: combination, mass, whole

ALACRITY
(uh-LA-kruh-tee)

. . . .

ALCHEMY
(AL-kuh-mee)

. . . .

ALLAY
(uh-LEY)

A

cheerful readiness

*He replied to the invitation with **alacrity**; he was eager for the opportunity to travel to Puerto Rico.*

Synonyms: liveliness, promptness, willingness

• •

the power or process that can change something ordinary into something valuable; a medieval pseudoscience with the purpose of changing lead into gold

*The **alchemy** that transformed him into a dashingly handsome man in her eyes was love.*

Synonyms: enchantment, magic, sorcery

• •

to put to rest; to decrease in strength or difficulty

*After they heard the coyotes howling, nothing but the dawn could **allay** their fears.*

Synonyms: alleviate, calm, ease, lessen, relieve

ALLEVIATE
(uh-LEE-vee-eyt)

. . . .

ALLOY
(A-loi)

. . . .

ALLURE
(uh-LOOR)

A

to lessen the burden, make easier

*Her calm support did much to **alleviate** his difficulties with the task.*

Synonyms: allay, ease, lighten, relieve

. . . .

a mixture of two or more different things; literally, a mixture of two or more metals or of a metal and nonmetal

*Even sterling silver is actually an **alloy** of silver with another metal, usually copper.*

Synonyms: blend, combination, composite, compound

. . . .

(v.) to attract

*Only the possibility that his favorite singer might perform could **allure** him to attend the concert.*

Synonyms: charm, entice, tempt

(n.) that which attracts

*Easily nauseated, she could not see the **allure** of a roller coaster.*

Synonyms: appeal, charm

AMALGAMATE
(uh-MAL-guh-MEYT)

. . . .

AMBIGUOUS
(am-BI-gyoo-wuhs)

. . . .

AMBIVALENCE
(am-BI-vuh-luhns)

to mix or combine into one body

*The plan to **amalgamate** the two high schools was not well thought out, and the students did not easily unite into one school.*

Synonyms: blend, incorporate, integrate, merge

. . . .

ill-defined or uncertain; possible to be understood in different ways

*Her habitual sarcasm rendered her statement **ambiguous**; no one could tell if she really meant what she said.*

Synonyms: cryptic, enigmatic, indefinite, indeterminate

. . . .

uncertainty; the state of having two or more contradictory feelings about something at the same time

*His **ambivalence** about playing the piano went on for years, and he thought about quitting every day until he enrolled at the conservatory.*

Synonyms: doubt, indecision, uncertainty

AMELIORATE
(uh-MEEL-yuh-reyt)

. . . .

AMENABLE
(uh-ME-nuh-buhl)

. . . .

AMENITY
(uh-ME-nuh-tee)

GRE VOCABULARY

A

to get or make better

*Her illness was **ameliorated** by the fact that it permitted her finally to rest and get enough sleep.*

Synonyms: alleviate, improve, relieve

· ·

agreeable, willing, or submissive; answerable or legally responsible; able to be examined or tested

*Even though it would require him to redo much of the work he had done so far, he was **amenable** to the change in plans.*

Synonyms: cooperative, manageable; accountable

· ·

the quality of being agreeable; a feature that increases value or comfort

*He had become so used to the general **amenity** of the community that the rudeness of the grocery store clerk shocked him.*

Synonyms: charm, pleasantness; advantage, convenience

ANACHRONISM
(uh-NA-kruh-ni-zuhm)

. . . .

ANALOGOUS
(uh-NA-luh-guhs)

. . . .

ANARCHY
(A-nuhr-kee)

a person or thing that is out of place in time

*Her floor-length skirts and elaborately done up hair were **anachronisms** that she nevertheless pulled off with grace.*

Synonym: misplacement

· ·

comparable in such a way that an analogy can be drawn

*Freud viewed the mind as **analogous** to a steam engine, whereas today we are more likely to compare it to a computer.*

Synonyms: alike, corresponding

· ·

lack of government; complete disorder

*When the teacher was called out of the classroom, the children erupted into gleeful **anarchy**.*

Synonyms: chaos, confusion, turmoil

ANATHEMA
(uh-NA-thuh-muh)

· ·

ANODYNE
(A-nuh-dahyn)

· ·

ANOMALY
(uh-NO-muh-lee)

A

someone or something that is cursed or disliked intensely; a curse

*Except for carrots, vegetables were **anathema** to the toddler.*

Synonyms: abomination, pariah

. . . .

something that comforts; a medicine that relieves pain

*The music of Bach was an **anodyne** to her through the months of mourning.*

Synonyms: balm; painkiller

. . . .

something different, irregular

*His late submission was an **anomaly**; he was known for meeting his deadlines.*

Synonyms: aberration, exception, irregularity, oddity

ANTIPATHY
(an-TI-puh-thee)

. . . .

APOSTATE
(uh-PO-steyt)

. . . .

APOGEE
(A-puh-jee)

A

A

dislike, feeling against

*He could not overcome his **antipathy** for dogs, even to date a woman who had a poodle as a pet.*

Synonyms: aversion, disgust, loathing

. . . .

one who renounces a previous loyalty, such as to a religion, nation, or party

*Though she had many disagreements with the party, she had no plans to become an **apostate.***

Synonyms: defector, dissenter, heretic, nonconformist

. . . .

the highest point; literally, the point at which an orbiting body is farthest from Earth

*Finalizing the deal that spring was the **apogee** of her career thus far.*

Synonyms: apex, climax, summit, zenith

APPEASE
(uh-PEEZ)

. . . .

APPRISE
(uh-PRAYHZ)

. . . .

APPROBATION
(a-pruh-BEY-shuhn)

to bring to a state of peace

*Only singing her favorite song could **appease** the distressed child.*

Synonyms: calm, pacify, soothe

. . . .

to inform

*He kept the radio on at all times, to be sure he was kept **apprised** of the latest weather report.*

Synonyms: advise, enlighten, notify

. . . .

formal approval

*Make art to express yourself, not to win the **approbation** of others.*

Synonyms: approval, commendation, endorsement, recognition

APPROPRIATE
(uh-PRO-pree-eyt)

. . . .

ARCHAIC
(ahr-KEY-ik)

. . . .

ARDUOUS
(AHR-juh-wuhs)

A

to set apart for a specific use; to take for oneself

*The army **appropriated** all vehicles in the region for military use.*

Synonyms: confiscate, seize, steal, usurp

. . . .

of the past; extremely old or out of date

*Students think that the language of Shakespeare is **archaic** until they encounter the work of Chaucer, who lived about two centuries earlier.*

Synonyms: ancient, obsolete, old-fashioned

. . . .

extremely difficult; requiring much energy or effort

*Running a marathon is **arduous** enough in itself; I can't imagine doing it as the last leg of a triathlon.*

Synonyms: exhausting, grueling, strenuous

ARTLESS
(AHRT-luhs)

....

ASCETIC
(uh-SE-tik)

....

ASPERITY
(a-SPER-uh-tee)

natural, simple, and without artificiality;
without knowledge or skill

*The child **artlessly** won over even the crankiest
adults simply by smiling at them.*

Synonyms: genuine, straightforward, unaffected,
uncultured

....

strictly self-denying, often for spiritual purposes

*The **ascetic** practices of a monk are certainly
not for everyone.*

Synonyms: austere, disciplined, strict

....

severity of tone, manner, or temper; roughness

*The **asperity** with which she spoke revealed
her anger about the situation.*

Synonyms: harshness, sharpness

ASPERSION
(uh-SPER-zhuhn)

....

ASSIDUOUS
(uh-SI-juh-wuhs)

....

ASSUAGE
(uh-SWEYJ)

A

a false accusation intended to do harm

*He cast **aspersions** on his rival, but everyone could see that his wild claims were not true.*

Synonyms: defamation, slander

. . . .

characterized by persistent and careful attention or effort

*An **assiduous** student, she earned the highest grades despite her learning disability.*

Synonyms: attentive, constant, persevering

. . . .

to decrease the intensity or severity of

*Nothing but time could **assuage** their grief after they lost their home.*

Synonyms: calm, ease, relieve

GRE VOCABULARY

ASTRINGENT
(uh-STRIN-juhnt)

. . . .

ASYLUM
(uh-SAHY-luhm)

. . . .

ATTENUATE
(uh-TEN-yuh-WEYT)

harsh, caustic, strict

*He was the only employee unafraid of the boss's **astringent** tongue.*

Synonyms: biting, bitter, cutting, sharp

. . . .

a place or state of shelter and protection; a place for the care of the ill or insane

*The refugees found **asylum** at the monastery.*

Synonyms: refuge, retreat, sanctuary

. . . .

to make thin or weak

*Her enthusiasm was **attenuated** by the length of the event; she did not like to be kept awake so late.*

Synonyms: debilitate, lessen, weaken

GRE VOCABULARY

AUDACIOUS
(aw-DEY-shuhs)

· ·

AUSTERE

(aw-STEER)

· ·

AUTONOMOUS
(aw-TO-nuh-muhs)

daring, recklessly brave; inventive, unconventional

*I am hardly **audacious** enough to go scuba diving, let alone sky diving!*

Synonyms: adventurous, bold, rash

. . . .

somber, strict, or stern in manner or appearance

*The house was plain and blended into the **austere** winter landscape.*

Synonyms: ascetic, rigorous, serious, solemn

. . . .

independent

*There are many who wish that the city government were more **autonomous** and did not have to abide by the decisions made at the distant state capital.*

Synonyms: self-governing, self-ruling, sovereign

AVARICE

(A-vuh-ruhs)

. . . .

AVER

(uh-VUHR)

. . . .

AVOCATION

(a-vuh-KEY-shun)

A

a greed for wealth that cannot be satisfied

His **avarice** was a source of great discontent; he could not be happy with what he already had.

Synonyms: covetousness, greed, rapacity

. . . .

to declare or prove to be true

I can **aver** that her story is true, because I was there and saw it happen myself.

Synonyms: affirm, assert, claim, verify

. . . .

an occupation pursued for enjoyment

She pursued her **avocation** of designing jewelry in the evenings after returning home from her day job.

Synonyms: diversion, hobby, pastime

AXIOMATIC
(AK-see-uh-MA-tik)

. . . .

A

taken as an axiom, or self-evident truth

*Until Copernicus showed otherwise, it was taken as **axiomatic** that the Earth was the center of the universe.*

Synonyms: accepted, fundamental, given, obvious

BANAL
(buh-NAL)

. . . .

BAWDY
(BAW-dee)

. . . .

BEHEMOTH
(bi-HEE-muhth)

B

unoriginal, trite

*The musical was unbelievably **banal**; the characters, plot, and music completely lacked originality.*

Synonyms: bland, conventional, hackneyed

. . . .

obscene, often in a boisterous or humorous way

*Shakespeare's language can be as **bawdy** as it is beautiful.*

Synonyms: coarse, indecent, lewd, vulgar

. . . .

something enormous in size or power

*The company was a **behemoth**, associated with about 1,000 brands, some of them even competing with each other.*

Synonyms: beast, giant, leviathan, mammoth

BELIE
(bi-LAYH)

. . . .

BELLICOSE
(BEH-li-kohs)

. . . .

BENEFICENT
(buh-NE-fuh-suhnt)

to reveal the falsehood of, contradict

*His blushing face **belied** his claim that he did not care.*

Synonyms: disprove, negate, repudiate

. . . .

inclined or eager to fight

*The **bellicose** young man picked fights on the playground nearly every day.*

Synonyms: belligerent, combative, hostile, warlike

. . . .

doing good

*Every fall, they celebrated the **beneficent** Earth for its rich harvest.*

Synonyms: benevolent, generous, kind

BLANDISHMENT
(BLAN-dish-muhnt)

. . . .

BOLSTER
(BOHL-stuhr)

. . . .

BOMBASTIC
(bom-BAS-tik)

flattery intended to persuade

*The **blandishments** of the salesperson got the better of her judgment, and she purchased the stereo, only to return it the next day.*

Synonyms: coaxing, fawning, wheedling

. . . .

to give support

*The coach **bolstered** their spirits after they played a poor first half, and ultimately they won the game.*

Synonyms: brace, sustain, uphold

. . . .

obnoxiously pretentious in speech or writing

*After an evening of listening to **bombastic** speeches, I left the award ceremony with a headache.*

Synonyms: pompous

BOORISH
(BOOR-ish)

. . . .

BRAZEN
(BREY-zuhn)

. . . .

BROACH
(brohch)

B

rude in a way that reveals insensitivity to others

*He lost several friends because of his **boorish** behavior at the party that night.*

Synonyms: bad mannered, coarse, crude

. . . .

shamelessly bold

*He was so **brazen** as to interrupt the guest speaker in the middle of her remarks.*

Synonyms: audacious, cocky, impudent

. . . .

to mention for the first time

*Though he loved her dearly, he was too timid to **broach** the topic of marriage.*

Synonyms: introduce, propose, suggest

BUCOLIC
(byoo-KO-lik)

. . . .

BURGEON
(BUHR-juhn)

. . . .

BURNISH
(BUHR-nish)

having to do with shepherds or rural life

He enjoyed their vacation in **bucolic** *northern New England; she longed to return to the city.*

Synonyms: pastoral, rural, rustic

. . . .

to sprout, bloom, and grow

She **burgeoned** *into an eager reader shortly after beginning first grade.*

Synonyms: blossom, flourish

. . . .

to polish, especially by rubbing

The carpenter **burnished** *the surface of the table until it was smooth and glossy.*

Synonyms: brighten, rub, shine

BUTTRESS
(BUH-truhs)

. . . .

to support, prop up

She listened to the anthem again and again, to **buttress** *her courage.*

Synonyms: bolster, brace, strengthen

CACOPHONY
(kuh-KO-fuh-nee)

. . . .

CALUMNY
(kuh-LUM-nee)

. . . .

CANON
(KA-nuhn)

harsh, discordant sound

*To her, it was powerfully stirring music; to her parents, it was unbearable **cacophony**.*

Synonyms: discord, noise

. . . .

false charges made with the intention of harming the reputation of another

*Despite the falseness of the charges, the **calumny** ended her career in politics.*

Synonyms: defamation, slander

. . . .

a body of fundamental rules or standards; a set of sacred texts or other comprehensive list of texts

*Many of the books we take as part of the **canon** today may be forgotten in the next century.*

Synonyms: dogma, law, principle

CANT
(kant)

. . . .

CAPRICIOUS
(kuhp-REE-shuhs)

. . . .

CAPTIOUS
(KAP-shuhs)

the use of trite or stock language, especially for insincere expressions of enthusiasm or piety

We were disgusted with the empty **cant** *of the politicians, who had done nothing to prevent the disaster.*

Synonyms: hypocrisy, sanctimoniousness

. . . .

impulsive, tending to act according to whim

He was so **capricious** *that he rarely kept a job longer than a few months.*

Synonyms: arbitrary, erratic, unpredictable

. . . .

tending to find fault; designed to confuse

The teacher's feedback was more **captious** *than instructive.*

Synonyms: cantankerous, faultfinding, finicky, nit-picking

CASTIGATION
(kas-ti-GEY-shuhn)

. . . .

CATALYST
(KA-tuh-luhst)

. . . .

CAUSAL
(KAW-zuhl)

severe criticism or punishment

*The children did not expect such **castigation** from their gentle teacher, who later apologized for reprimanding them so harshly.*

Synonyms: chastisement, discipline, invective

. . . .

an agent that causes or speeds up a change or activity; literally, a substance that causes or speeds up a chemical reaction

*They had talked about moving for years; her pregnancy was the **catalyst** that finally spurred them to take action.*

Synonyms: impetus, stimulus

. . . .

relating to a cause

*She understood the **causal** relationship between the care she took with her studies and her grades.*

CAUSTIC
(KAWS-tik)

. . . .

CAVIL
(KA-vil)

. . . .

CENSURE
(SEN-sher)

C

able to burn or corrode; sarcastic

Her **caustic** tone and sarcastic words said
everything we needed to know about her
thoughts about getting fired.

Synonyms: acerbic, biting, harsh

• •

to raise minor objections

His tendency to **cavil** at new ideas made him a
poor manager, and he was soon fired.

Synonyms: criticize, quibble

• •

blame, formal condemnation

The **censure** of her colleagues did nothing to
curb her illicit behavior.

Synonyms: criticism, disapproval, reprimand

CHARY
(CHER-ee)

. . . .

CHASTEN
(CHEY-suhn)

. . . .

CHICANERY
(shi-KEYN-uh-ree)

C

cautious

*She was **chary** of auditioning for another play after the last production ended in a debacle.*

Synonyms: careful, restrained, wary

• •

to correct through punishment

*The children were thoroughly **chastened** after they spent their weekend cleaning the playground they had damaged.*

Synonyms: discipline, humiliate, subdue

• •

deception through trickery

*He won the competition through **chicanery**, not talent.*

Synonyms: artifice, cheating, subterfuge

CHIMERA
(kahy-MIR-uh)

. . . .

CIRCUITOUS
(suhr-KYOO-uh-tuhs)

. . . .

COAGULATE
(koh-A-gyuh-leyt)

C

a terrible illusion, an imagined monster

*The **chimera** that haunts him at night is his idea of himself in the future.*

Synonyms: delusion, mirage

• •

going in a winding, indirect way

*Though it may have been quicker to go by the highway, we enjoyed the **circuitous** drive to the lake.*

Synonyms: rambling, roundabout

• •

to thicken; to gather in a mass

*The milk became sour and began to **coagulate**.*

Synonyms: congeal, clot, curdle, solidify

CODA
(KOH-duh)

. . . .

COGENT
(KOH-juhnt)

. . . .

COMMENSURATE
(kuh-MEN-se-ruht)

the conclusion of a work of music, literature, drama, or film, often formally different from the rest of the work

*We knew how the story was going to turn out long before the play reached its **coda**.*

Synonyms: conclusion, ending, finale

. . . .

very convincing and appealing to reason; relevant

*The senator was not able to give a **cogent** argument in favor of his re-election.*

Synonyms: apt, compelling, persuasive, telling

. . . .

equal or corresponding in measure, degree, intensity, or duration

*If your effort is **commensurate** with your desire, you are likely to succeed.*

Synonyms: comparable, equivalent, proportionate

COMPENDIUM
(kuhm-PEN-dee-uhm)

· ·

COMPLACENT
(kuhm-PLEY-suhnt)

· ·

COMPLAISANT
(kuhm-PLEY-suhnt)

a summary of a larger work or body of knowledge; a complete list of items

The thin volume included a **compendium** *of all the different kinds of birds he had seen visiting the woods in his backyard.*

Synonyms: abstract, digest, overview, survey

. . . .

satisfied with one's own condition

It is easy to be **complacent** *with one's own good fortune rather than to use it to better the lives of others.*

Synonyms: self-satisfied, smug, unconcerned

. . . .

inclined to please

The girl was shy but **complaisant**, *and soon warmed up to the company.*

Synonyms: agreeable, gracious, obliging

COMPLEMENT
(KOM-pluh-ment)

· ·

COMPLIANT
(kuhm-PLAHY-uhnt)

· ·

CONCILIATORY
(kuhn-SI-lee-uh-taw-ree)

C

something that completes or perfects

*For her, coffee is a necessary **complement** to breakfast.*

Synonyms: counterpart, enhancement, supplement

. . . .

conforming, submissive

*Stand firmly on your ground—don't be so **compliant**!*

Synonyms: docile, obedient, obliging, yielding

. . . .

tending to gain goodwill, overcome distrust

*Upon hearing her **conciliatory** words, no one was in the mood to argue anymore.*

Synonyms: appeasing, civil, placating

CONFOUND
(kuhn-FOUND)

. . . .

CONNOISSEUR
(ko-nuh-SUHR)

. . . .

CONTENTION
(kuhn-TEN-shuhn)

to confuse thoroughly

*The directions **confounded** her so completely that she ended up on the wrong side of town.*

Synonyms: baffle, bewilder, frustrate, perplex

. . . .

one who understands, appreciates, and can make judgments of an art or matter of taste

*Though he claimed to be a **connoisseur** of twentieth century art, he could not even tell a Picasso from a Pollock.*

Synonyms: aficionado, expert, specialist

. . . .

opposition, strife; an idea proposed and held in debate or argument

*The constant mishaps of her lackadaisical brother became a source of **contention** with her husband.*

Synonyms: conflict, discord, quarrel

CONTIGUOUS
(kuhn-TI-gyoo-wuhs)

. . . .

CONTRITE
(kuhn-TRAHYT)

. . . .

CONTUMACIOUS
(kon-too-MEY-shuhs)

C

in contact, adjoining

*The state of Alaska is **contiguous** with Canada but not with the United States.*

Synonyms: adjacent, bordering, neighboring, touching

• •

feeling or showing sorrow for wrongdoing

*Though he was **contrite** after their argument, she was not easily willing to forgive.*

Synonyms: apologetic, penitent, remorseful, sorry

• •

stubbornly rebellious

*The **contumacious** little girl refused to listen to reason and to wear a jacket or shoes.*

Synonyms: headstrong, obstinate

CONUNDRUM
(kuh-NUHN-druhm)

. . . .

CONVENTION
(kuhn-VEN-shuhn)

. . . .

CONVIVIAL
(kuhn-VI-vee-uhl)

C

a complicated problem; literally, a riddle with a pun or wordplay in its answer

*The disorder in his bedroom every morning was a **conundrum**, until they realized that he was sleepwalking at night.*

Synonyms: puzzle, riddle, trick

• •

a meeting; an agreement; the standard or usual way of doing things

*As e-mail has become the main form of written correspondence, many people are forgetting the **conventions** of letter writing.*

Synonyms: custom, habit

• •

enjoying company, food, and drink

*A **convivial** person, she looks forward to the holidays even though they mark the beginning of winter.*

Synonyms: agreeable, friendly, jovial

CONVOLUTED
(KON-vuh-loo-tuhd)

....

COPIOUS
(KOH-pee-uhs)

....

CRAVEN
(KREY-vuhn)

full of twists and turns, complicated

*His **convoluted** directions were unnecessary; all that he needed to say was, "Turn left at the corner."*

Synonyms: complex, intricate, puzzling

. . . .

numerous, plentiful

*She took **copious** notes and filled several notebooks every term.*

Synonyms: abundant, extensive, generous

. . . .

completely lacking in courage

*Please tell me you are not so **craven** as to forfeit the game rather than face your fiercest opponent.*

Synonyms: cowardly, fearful, timid

CREDULOUS
(KRE-juh-luhs)

. . . .

CULPABLE
(KUHL-puh-buhl)

. . . .

CYNICISM
(SI-nuh-si-zuhm)

willing to believe; originating in credulity

*As a teacher, he was far too **credulous**, and his students could get away with almost anything, so long as they could tell a story to explain it.*

Synonyms: believing, gullible, unsuspecting

• •

deserving blame

*Though she was clearly **culpable**, she was never even charged for the crime.*

Synonyms: blameworthy, guilty, liable

• •

a complete lack of faith, especially in the values and motives of humans

*Despite his **cynicism**, he was also charming, and soon everyone was seduced by his gloomy outlook.*

Synonyms: bitterness, negativism, pessimism, sarcasm

CYNOSURE
(SI-no-shor)

. . . .

center of attraction

*The movie star is an unapologetic **cynosure**; she always expects all eyes to be on her.*

Synonyms: hotshot

DEARTH
(duhrth)

. . . .

DEBACLE
(duh-BAH-kuhl)

. . . .

DEBAUCHERY
(di-BAW-chuh-ree)

a shortage, an inadequate supply

*The **dearth** of clean water was due to the drought.*

Synonyms: deficiency, lack, scarcity

· ·

a disaster or complete failure

*The play was supposed to be a tragedy, but the production was such a **debacle** that the audience laughed through the third act.*

Synonyms: breakdown, defeat, fiasco, wreck

· ·

indulgence in physical pleasures

*His life of **debauchery** took a toll on his body, and he looked far older than his years.*

Synonyms: depravity, intemperance, revelry

GRE VOCABULARY

DECORUM
(di-KOHR-uhm)

. . . .

DEFAULT
(di-FAWLT)

. . . .

DEFERENCE
(DEH-fuh-ruhns)

D

propriety and good taste

Please conduct yourselves with **decorum** *during our visit to the mayor's office.*

Synonyms: civility, convention, dignity

. . . .

(n.) a failure to act or fulfill an obligation

We hired him by **default**; *none of the other applicants showed up for the interview.*

Synonyms: disregard, neglect

(v.) to fail to act or fulfill an obligation

She **defaulted** *on her mortgage payments after she lost her job.*

Synonyms: evade, neglect

. . . .

respect for and submission to the judgment or will of another, especially an elder or superior

The children treated their grandparents with **deference**.

Synonyms: compliance, courtesy, esteem, regard

DEFUNCT
(di-FUHNGKT)

. . . .

DELINEATE
(di-LI-nee-eyt)

. . . .

DEMUR

(di-MUHR)

GRE VOCABULARY

D

no longer working or in use; no longer existing

*The organization had been **defunct** for nearly a decade when she decided to revive it.*

Synonyms: obsolete; extinct

. . . .

to describe or portray in detail

*The CEO took the time to **delineate** her plans for the company, so that everyone would understand the direction they would be taking in the next year.*

Synonyms: characterize, depict, draw, represent

. . . .

to express disagreement, object

*Everyone else was enthusiastic about the project, but she **demurred**, saying it would never succeed.*

Synonyms: oppose, refuse

DENIGRATE
(de-ni-GREYT)

. . . .

DENOUEMENT
(DEY-noo-mawn)

. . . .

DERISION
(di-RI-zhuhn)

D

D

to attack the reputation or achievements of another

*He did nothing but **denigrate** his classmates' artwork, but could hardly tolerate the most neutral comment about his own.*

Synonyms: belittle, criticize, disparage

. . . .

the outcome of a story or series of events

*The **denouement** was unsatisfying: the hero woke up, and it turned out that the entire story had been his dream.*

Synonyms: conclusion, culmination, resolution

. . . .

ridicule, contempt

*The poorly plotted film was the object of much **derision** from critics, but audiences loved it.*

Synonyms: disdain, mockery, scorn

DERIVATIVE
(di-RI-vuh-tiv)

. . . .

DESICCATE
(DEH-si-keyt)

. . . .

DESUETUDE
(DEH-swi-tood)

D

derived from something else, lacking in originality

*His first album was **derivative** R & B, but his second album was completely original and propelled him to fame.*

Synonyms: banal, copied, imitative

· ·

to dry up

*The **desiccated** landscape had not seen rain in months.*

Synonyms: dehydrate, deplete, wither

· ·

the state of no longer being in use

*After the original members of the sorority graduated, many of their rituals were forgotten and soon fell into **desuetude**.*

Synonyms: disuse, inactivity

GRE VOCABULARY

DESULTORY
(DE-suhl-tohr-ee)

. . . .

DETERRENT
(di-TUHR-uhnt)

. . . .

DETRACTION
(di-TRAK-shuhn)

lacking a plan or sense of purpose, disconnected

*His **desultory** ways were maddening to her; she preferred to get right to the point.*

Synonyms: aimless, chance, erratic, rambling

· ·

that which prevents

*The new methods of policing the neighborhood turned out to be an effective **deterrent** to crime.*

Synonyms: curb, hindrance, obstacle, restraint

· ·

a lessening of reputation, especially due to criticism; the act of taking away

*As a result of the critics' many **detractions** of the novel, it sold only a few dozen copies.*

Synonyms: misrepresentation, slander

DIAPHANOUS
(dahy-A-fuh-nuhs)

....

DIATRIBE
(DAHY-uh-trahyb)

....

DICHOTOMY
(dahy-KO-tuh-mee)

D

extremely fine or delicate to the point of transparency; insubstantial

*The starlet's **diaphanous** gown was both gorgeous and scandalous.*

Synonyms: gossamer, flimsy, sheer

. . . .

a critical or abusive speech or piece of writing

*After taking in her boss's long **diatribe** about her work, she simply quit.*

Synonyms: harangue, invective, tirade

. . . .

a division into two opposite or mutually exclusive groups

*The **dichotomy** between her words and actions was startling; to hear her talk, you'd think she could do nothing right, whereas I had never seen her do anything wrong.*

Synonyms: bifurcation, difference, separation

DIDACTIC
(dahy-DAK-tik)

. . . .

DIFFIDENCE
(DI-fi-duhns)

. . . .

DIFFUSE
(di-FYOOS)

D

tending or intended to inform or teach

*Because our values are so different today, the **didactic** novels of the past are now more humorous than instructive.*

Synonyms: academic, instructive, pendantic

. . . .

shyness, lack of confidence

*He overcame his **diffidence** and gave a stirring speech at the rally.*

Synonyms: hesitancy, insecurity, reluctance, reservation

. . . .

wordy and disorganized; not concentrated, spread around

*The lecturer was so **diffuse** that although she shared a wealth of information, we hardly learned anything.*

Synonyms: rambling; diluted, scattered, widespread

GRE VOCABULARY

DIGRESSION
(dahy-GRE-shuhn)

. . . .

DILETTANTE
(DI-luh-tahnt)

. . . .

DIRGE
(duhrj)

a turning away from the main course or subject

*This paragraph is a **digression** from the main topic of the essay, but it is more interesting to me than anything else.*

Synonyms: departure, diversion, wandering

. . . .

a lover of or dabbler in the arts

*He called himself a **dilettante**, but he was actually an accomplished pianist.*

Synonyms: amateur, connoisseur, rookie

. . . .

a slow, mournful piece of music, especially one intended for a funeral or similar occasion

*The orchestra played the piece so slowly that it sounded like a **dirge**.*

Synonyms: lament, requiem

DISABUSE
(DIS-uh-byooz)

. . . .

DISCERNING
(di-SUHR-ning)

. . . .

DISCORDANT
(dis-KOR-duhnt)

to clear up an error or confusion

*The nutritionist worked hard to **disabuse** the public of the notion that vegetarians cannot get enough protein.*

Synonyms: correct, debunk, enlighten

. . . .

having good judgment or understanding

*Only the most **discerning** customers can tell the difference between this fabric and real silk.*

Synonyms: discriminating, insightful, knowledgeable, perceptive

. . . .

not in harmony, quarrelsome

*She was a brilliant leader who could listen to the **discordant** voices of the Senate and somehow find a way to compromise.*

Synonyms: cacophonous, contradictory, inconsistent

DISCREDIT
(dis-KRE-duht)

. . . .

DISCREET
(dis-KREET)

. . . .

DISCREPANCY
(dis-KRE-puhn-see)

to refuse to believe or cause others to disbelieve

*He had to **discredit** the ridiculous idea that with a better diet, one could get by with only five hours of sleep each night.*

Synonyms: doubt, question, reject

. . . .

maintaining or respecting privacy, especially about something of a delicate nature

*They were so **discreet** about the affair that it was never discovered.*

Synonyms: cautious, modest, prudent, restrained

. . . .

disagreement, inconsistency

*The investigation of a small **discrepancy** in an account revealed widespread fraud at that bank.*

Synonyms: conflict, difference, dissimilarity, variation

DISCRETE
(dis-KREET)

. . . .

DISINGENUOUS
(dis-in-JEN-yoo-uhs)

. . . .

DISINTERESTED
(dis-IN-truhs-tuhd)

GRE VOCABULARY

D

separate, distinct

*The course was given in three **discrete** sessions; you could attend just one or two and still follow the material.*

Synonyms: apart, detached, isolated

. . . .

lacking in truth, often while giving the appearance of truthfulness

*Their advertising was **disingenuous**, featuring photographs that made their dumpy hotel look like a paradise.*

Synonyms: deceitful, dishonest, insincere, hypocritical

. . . .

not personally engaged, without emotional interest

*He could not participate on the jury; the victim was his cousin, and so he could not be **disinterested** in the outcome of the trial.*

Synonyms: dispassionate, indifferent, unbiased, unconcerned

DISJOINTED
(dis-JOIN-tuhd)

. . . .

DISMISS
(dis-MIS)

. . . .

DISPARAGE
(di-SPER-ij)

disorderly, out of sequence

*She told the story in such a **disjointed** way that we asked her to repeat it so that we could understand.*

Synonyms: confused, disconnected, incoherent, rambling

. . . .

to allow or cause to leave; to reject

*She **dismissed** the proposal, saying that it would be too expensive to carry out.*

Synonyms: discharge, release, send away; disregard

. . . .

to speak of slightingly; to lessen the reputation of

*Do not **disparage** your elders; they worked hard to build this community.*

Synonyms: belittle, depreciate

DISPARATE
(DIS-puhr-uht)

. . . .

DISSEMBLE
(di-SEM-buhl)

. . . .

DISSEMINATE
(di-SE-muh-neyt)

essentially different

*The four musicians brought together their **disparate** talents and ideas to make a wild and beautiful collection of songs.*

Synonyms: dissimilar, diverse, various

. . . .

to put on a false appearance

*The children tried to **dissemble** innocence, but the crumbs on their face gave them away.*

Synonyms: conceal, feign, simulate

. . . .

to scatter, spread around

*Please **disseminate** the news; I want everyone to know about my candidacy.*

Synonyms: advertise, broadcast, disperse, publish

DISSIDENT
(DI-suh-duhnt)

. . . .

DISSOLUTION
(DI-suh-loo-shuhn)

. . . .

DISSONANCE
(DI-suh-nuhns)

disagreeing with an established belief or organization

*Under the rule of the dictator, people kept their **dissident** ideas to themselves.*

Synonyms: heretical, nonconforming, unorthodox

· ·

the act or process of falling apart

*The **dissolution** of their marriage was unexpected; they had seemed so happy.*

Synonyms: disintegration, rupture, separation

· ·

the clashing of ideas or sounds

*The music included much **dissonance**, and I left the concert hall with a headache.*

Synonyms: conflict, disagreement, discord

DISTEND
(dis-TEND)

. . . .

DISTILL
(dis-TIL)

. . . .

DIVEST
(dahy-VEST)

to expand, swell

*Ironically, their **distended** bellies are a sign of their great hunger.*

Synonyms: bloat, bulge, enlarge

. . . .

to extract the essence of

*The professor could **distill** complex ideas into a simple diagram or statement.*

Synonyms: concentrate, purify, refine

. . . .

to strip, deprive, or free from

*He **divested** himself of most of his wealth and went off to live in the woods.*

Synonyms: dismantle, dispossess, seize

GRE VOCABULARY

DIVULGE
(dahy-VUHLJ)

. . . .

DOCTRINAIRE
(dok-truh-NAIR)

. . . .

DOGMATIC
(dawg-MA-tik)

D

to make a secret known

*She refused to **divulge** what her sister had told her that evening.*

Synonyms: admit, disclose, tell

. . . .

fanatic about a doctrine or theory

*A **doctrinaire** libertarian, she refused to pay any taxes.*

Synonyms: dogmatic, fanatical, impractical, inflexible

. . . .

taken to expressing opinions as though they were facts

*She was turned off by his **dogmatic** assertions that reading his book would completely transform her life.*

Synonyms: fanatical, opinionated

DORMANT
(DAWR-muhnt)

. . . .

DROSS
(dros)

. . . .

DUPE
(doop)

D

inactive, asleep

It is hard to believe that the tulip bulbs lie **dormant** *in the earth under the winter snow.*

Synonyms: inert, latent, potential

. . . .

waste, something that is inferior

The art show was so full of **dross** *that his beautiful piece stood out.*

Synonyms: refuse, scum, trash

. . . .

one who is easily deceived or fooled

He was a **dupe** *to believe all of her lies.*

Synonyms: chump, fool

EBULLIENT
(i-BOOL-yuhnt)

. . . .

ECCENTRIC
(ek-SEN-trik)

. . . .

ECLECTIC
(e-KLEK-tik)

E

lively, enthusiastic

*We soon were all carried away by her **ebullient** mood.*

Synonyms: buoyant, high-spirited, vivacious

. . . .

unconventional, irregular

*Her staid outfits contrasted with her **eccentric** ideas.*

Synonyms: odd, unusual, whimsical

. . . .

choosing from a variety of sources; composed of a variety of styles, methods, or ideas

*His taste in music was **eclectic**, including everything from opera to free jazz.*

Synonyms: assorted, diverse, varied

EFFERVESCENCE
(e-fuhr-VE-sens)

. . . .

EFFETE
(e-FEET)

. . . .

EFFICACY
(EH-fi-kuh-see)

E

liveliness

*Her **effervescence** was not appropriate for the solemn occasion.*

Synonyms: enthusiasm, excitement

. . . .

without strength or character

*The young men longed for war so that they could prove they had not grown **effete**.*

Synonyms: decadent, degenerate, sterile

. . . .

the ability to produce the desired effect

*Her **efficacy** was astonishing; within three days she got the project back on track.*

Synonyms: capability, competence, effectiveness

EFFRONTERY
(i-FRUHN-tuh-ree)

. . . .

ELEGY
(E-luh-jee)

. . . .

ELICIT
(i-LI-suht)

E

shameless boldness

*He had the **effrontery** to demand a full refund, simply because he had not liked one of the performers.*

Synonyms: arrogance, disrespect, insolence

. . . .

a poem or song expressing sorrow at the loss of one who has died

*After the poet read the **elegy** for her mother, not an eye was dry of tears.*

Synonyms: lament, requiem

. . . .

to draw or bring out

*Her pointed questions **elicited** thoughtful replies.*

Synonyms: evoke, obtain

ELIXIR
(i-LIK-suhr)

. . . .

ELOQUENT
(EH-luh-kwuhnt)

. . . .

EMACIATED
(i-MEY-shee-ey-tuhd)

E

a sweetened mixture of alcohol and water having medicinal qualities

*He made a fortune selling an **elixir** that he claimed could preserve youth.*

Synonyms: medicine, solution

· ·

beautifully and fluently expressive

*She wrote an **eloquent** letter to thank her aunt for the gift.*

Synonyms: articulate, expressive

· ·

made thin and week

*The cat was **emaciated** when we found her, but now she is healthy though a bit plump.*

Synonyms: haggard, skinny, starved, wasted

EMBELLISH
(im-BE-lish)

· ·

EMOLLIENT
(i-MOL-yuhnt)

· ·

EMPIRICAL
(im-PIR-i-kuhl)

to add ornamentation

*He **embellished** the story with little exaggerations to make it more interesting.*

Synonyms: adorn, decorate, enhance

· ·

having the power to soothe or make soft and supple

*The midwife's **emollient** words encouraged the woman in labor.*

Synonyms: healing, soothing; lotion, salve

· ·

based on observation or experience without resorting to theory

*Your arguments are too theoretical; only **empirical** evidence will persuade me.*

Synonyms: experimental, observed, practical

EMULATE
(EM-yuh-leyt)

. . . .

ENCOMIUM
(en-KOH-mee-uhm)

. . . .

ENDEMIC
(en-DEM-ik)

to try to equal or excel; to imitate

*He had no desire to **emulate** his novelist father and instead became an accountant.*

Synonyms: compete, follow, rival

. . . .

praise, an expression of praise

*The **encomium** from all the critics in the world did not matter so much to her as the praise her teacher heaped on her little book.*

Synonyms: accolade, tribute

. . . .

characteristic of or prevalent in a group of people or region

*The Joshua tree is **endemic** to the Mojave Desert; it grows nowhere else.*

Synonyms: aboriginal, local, regional

ENERVATE
(E-nuhr-veyt)

· ·

ENGENDER
(en-JEN-duhr)

· ·

ENHANCE
(en-HANS)

to reduce the strength of

*The heat and humidity **enervated** her so much that she did not even try to accomplish anything on that day.*

Synonyms: debilitate, enfeeble, weaken

. . . .

to bring into existence

*His unclear directions **engendered** confusion.*

Synonyms: beget, generate, originate, produce

. . . .

to improve in quality, desirability, or value

*Her new hairstyle did much to **enhance** her appearance.*

Synonyms: augment, embellish, improve, intensify

ENIGMATIC
(e-nig-MA-tik)

. . . .

ENNUI
(ahn-WEE)

. . . .

ENUNCIATE
(ee-NUHN-see-eyt)

puzzling, mysterious

*He lay in bed that night trying to sort out the meaning of her **enigmatic** good-bye.*

Synonyms: ambiguous, perplexing

. . . .

a feeling of weariness

*Despite the wealth of opportunities available to me, I could not shake the feeling of **ennui** at the very thought of starting another job.*

Synonyms: boredom, dullness, languor

. . . .

to pronounce clearly; to announce

*I will **enunciate** my intentions only after my plans are settled.*

Synonyms: articulate; declare, proclaim

EPHEMERAL
(i-FEM-uh-ruhl)

. . . .

EQUANIMITY
(e-kwuh-NI-muh-tee)

. . . .

EQUIVOCATE
(i-KWI-vuh-keyt)

lasting a short time

*Pleasure may be **ephemeral**, but so is pain.*

Synonyms: brief, fleeting, momentary, passing

. . . .

mental stability under stress

*The secret to her **equanimity** was that no matter how much she had to do, she always got enough sleep.*

Synonyms: calmness, composure, equilibrium, serenity

. . . .

to speak without committing oneself

*When I ask this next question, don't **equivocate**; just say directly what is on your mind.*

Synonyms: dodge, evade, prevaricate

GRE VOCABULARY

ERRANT
(EH-ruhnt)

. . . .

ERUDITE
(ER-yuh-dahyt)

. . . .

ESCHEW
(e-SHOO)

given to wandering; tending to err

The **errant** child soon lost her way.

Synonyms: meandering, rambling, straying; fallible

. . . .

learned

The professor was **erudite**, not only in her own field of scholarship but also in twentieth-century poetry.

Synonyms: educated, knowledgeable, studious

. . . .

to avoid, especially for ethical or practical reasons

A strict vegetarian, she **eschews** eggs and dairy products in addition to meat and fish.

Synonyms: abstain, renounce, shun

ESSAY
(e-SEY)

. . . .

ESOTERIC
(e-suh-TEH-rik)

. . . .

ESTIMABLE
(ES-tuh-muh-buhl)

E

to attempt, to try

*I have **essayed** neither rock climbing nor sky diving, and probably never will try either activity.*

Synonyms: test, undertake

. . . .

known only by the initiated

*The symbolism of the Tarot is hardly as **esoteric** as you might think.*

Synonyms: arcane, hidden, occult

. . . .

capable of being estimated; worthy of respect

*We practiced hard that week to prepare to face an **estimable** opponent.*

Synonyms: admirable, reputable, respectable

EULOGY
(YOO-luh-jee)

. . . .

EUPHEMISM
(YOO-fuh-mi-zuhm)

. . . .

EVANESCENT
(e-vuh-NEH-suhnt)

E

a speech or piece of writing given in honor of someone who has died

*Each of his five sons gave a brief and moving **eulogy** at his funeral.*

Synonyms: tribute

. . . .

the use of a neutral or vague word or phrase to replace a word or phrase that might offend or seem harsh or unpleasant

*"To pass away" is a common **euphemism** for "to die."*

Synonyms: circumlocution, delicacy, pretense

. . . .

like vapor, tending to fade or vanish

*Young people do not know just how **evanescent** youth is.*

Synonyms: fleeting, passing, temporary, transient

EVINCE
(i-VINS)

. . . .

EVOCATIVE
(i-VO-kuh-tiv)

. . . .

EXACERBATE
(ig-ZA-suhr-beyt)

E

to give evidence of, reveal

*That he was able to read when he was only three years old **evinced** his intelligence and eagerness to learn.*

Synonyms: demonstrate, display, indicate, manifest, show

. . . .

tending to call forth or suggest emotion or ideas

*Though the paintings were abstract, they were **evocative** of desert landscapes.*

Synonyms: expressive, suggestive

. . . .

to make worse

*The couple was deep in debt, and so the loss of her job only **exacerbated** their problems.*

Synonyms: aggravate, infuriate, intensify

EXACT
(ig-ZAKT)

. . . .

EXECRABLE
(EK-si-kruh-buhl)

. . . .

EXCULPATE
(EK-skuhl-peyt)

E

to call for and obtain, demand

*The coach was so successful because she **exacted** the best effort from her teams.*

Synonyms: compel, require

. . . .

detestable, very bad

*He was sentenced to a life in prison for his **execrable** crimes.*

Synonyms: abominable, disgusting, horrible, loathsome

. . . .

to clear from guilt or blame

*Not only was she **exculpated** of the charge that she had cheated on the test, but her teacher apologized profusely.*

Synonyms: absolve, exonerate, vindicate

EXHORT
(ig-ZORT)

. . . .

EXISTENTIAL
(eg-zi-STEN-shuhl)

. . . .

EXIGENCY
(EK-suh-juhn-see)

E

to advise or urge strongly

*Though he **exhorted** his students to attend his evening study sessions, they were poorly attended.*

Synonyms: admonish, beseech, encourage, recommend

. . . .

having to do with being and existence

*The philosopher's concerns were **existential**; she questioned how and why human life came to be.*

. . . .

that which is necessary in a given situation; an urgent situation

*He was ill prepared for the **exigencies** of life abroad.*

Synonyms: necessity, requirement; crisis, emergency

EXONERATE
(ig-ZO-nuh-reyt)

· ·

EXPIATE
(EK-spee-eyt)

· ·

EXPLICATE
(EKS-pli-keyt)

E

to clear from blame; to relieve of a responsibility

*We were relieved to be **exonerated** of our cleaning duties that weekend.*

Synonyms: absolve, exonerate, vindicate; discharge, liberate

. . . .

to make amends

*To **expiate** for their vandalism, they painted a beautiful mural over the graffiti.*

Synonyms: atone, compensate, rectify

. . . .

to explain in detail

*In her term paper, she **explicated** the meaning of The Rime of the Ancient Mariner by Samuel Taylor Coleridge.*

Synonyms: analyze, clarify, interpret

EXPOSITORY
(ik-SPO-zuh-taw-ree)

. . . .

EXTEMPORANEOUS
(ek-stem-puh-REY-nee-uhs)

. . . .

EXTIRPATE
(EK-stuhr-peyt)

conveying information or explanations

*She enjoyed **expository** writing so much that she decided to pursue a career as a journalist.*

Synonyms: explanatory, informative

. . . .

made, done, or said at the spur of the moment

*His **extemporaneous** speech was both funnier and more moving than his colleague's carefully planned one.*

Synonyms: impromptu, improvised, unre-hearsed

. . . .

to destroy at the roots

*The new police chief was determined to **extirpate** crime from the city.*

Synonyms: annihilate, demolish, eradicate, exterminate, extinguish

EXTRANEOUS
(ek-STREY-nee-uhs)

. . . .

EXTRAPOLATE
(ik-STRA-puh-leyt)

. . . .

EXTRINSIC
(ek-STRIN-zik)

E

coming from without, extra

Address the main topic only; leave out any **extraneous** *details, however entertaining they might be.*

Synonyms: additional, external, foreign, superfluous, unessential

. . . .

to infer, predict, or project based on given information

Be careful not to **extrapolate** *too wildly from the survey results; stick close to the data.*

Synonyms: conclude, envision

. . . .

originating from without

The movie reminded the critic of his childhood, but he recognized that these memories were **extrinsic** *to the quality of the film itself.*

Synonyms: external, extraneous, unessential

FACETIOUS
(fuh-SEE-shuhs)

. . . .

FACILITATE
(fuh-SI-luh-teyt)

. . . .

FALLACY
(FA-luh-see)

GRE VOCABULARY

F

not serious, inappropriately jokey

The **facetious** tone of the guide regarding first aid was at odds with the serious of its purpose.

Synonyms: amusing, frivolous, humorous

. . . .

to make easier
To **facilitate** the discussion, please raise your hand if you wish to speak.

Synonyms: aid, assist, expedite, promote

. . . .

a deceptive or mistaken idea or belief

It is a **fallacy** to believe that humans evolved from chimpanzees; we do share a common ancestor, however.

Synonyms: delusion, error, misconception

FALLOW
(FA-loh)

. . . .

FATUOUS
(FA-choo-uhs)

. . . .

FAWNING
(FAW-ning)

F

left uncultivated, inactive

*The farmer let that field lie **fallow** this year so that it would not be depleted.*

Synonyms: dormant, idle, resting

. . . .

foolish

*His **fatuous** comments during the interview made him seem untrustworthy, and so he was not hired.*

Synonyms: idiotic, mindless, ridiculous, silly

. . . .

showing affection or seeking favor through flattery

*Unable to trust the **fawning** attitudes of those around her, the celebrity relied on her family and oldest friends.*

Synonyms: flattering, ingratiating, pandering

FELICITOUS
(fi-LI-suh-tuhs)

• •

FERVENT
(FUHR-vuhnt)

• •

FILIBUSTER
(FI-luh-buh-stuhr)

F

well expressed or well suited

Her **felicitous** remarks put the students at ease before the test.

Synonyms: apt, appropriate

. . . .

intense

His **fervent** admiration of her went unreturned; she found him uninteresting.

Synonyms: ardent, heartfelt, passionate

. . . .

the use of obstruction to prevent action, especially the passage of a law

Due to the **filibuster** by just one senator, there was no vote on the bill.

Synonyms: delay, hindrance, interference, opposition

FLAG
(flag)

. . . .

FLEDGLING
(FLEJ-ling)

. . . .

FLOUT
(flout)

to lose interest or spirit

*Seeing that their enthusiasm for the hike was **flagging**, the guide decided that it was time to take a break.*

Synonyms: dwindle, slump, wane

. . . .

a beginner

*I am learning Chinese, but I'm just a **fledgling** speaker, having studied the language for only six months.*

Synonyms: novice, rookie

. . . .

to neglect or treat with scorn

*She showed her disrespect for her teachers by **flouting** their rules.*

Synonyms: distain, disregard, insult

FOMENT
(foh-MENT)

. . . .

FORESTALL
(fohr-STAWL)

. . . .

FORTUITOUS
(fawr-TOO-uh-tuhs)

F

to promote the growth of

*The newspaper editor was accused of **fomenting** rebellion by publishing stories that were highly critical of the government.*

Synonyms: agitate, cultivate, encourage, foster

· ·

to hinder or delay

*The actions that the police took to **forestall** a riot might actually have caused it to occur.*

Synonyms: prevent, thwart

· ·

lucky, happening by a lucky chance

*The weather on the day of the marathon could not have been more **fortuitous**: partly cloudy and cool but not humid.*

Synonyms: accidental, fortunate

GRE VOCABULARY

FRACTIOUS
(FRAK-shuhs)

. . . .

FRUGALITY
(froo-GA-luh-tee)

. . . .

FULMINATE
(fuhl-muh-NEYT)

tending to be quarrelsome or troublesome

*The boys had a reputation for being **fractious**, but I never saw them be anything other than polite and well behaved.*

Synonyms: unruly, rebellious, wayward, wild

• •

the tendency to be sparing with money and other resources, not wasteful

*Her tendency to indulge in expensive shoes contrasted with her **frugality** in all other matters.*

Synonyms: conservation, economy, prudence

• •

to denounce strongly

*The preacher **fulminated** against gambling and other forms of idleness and waste.*

Synonyms: attack, condemn, criticize

GRE VOCABULARY

FULSOME
(FUHL-sum)

. . . .

FURTIVE
(FUHR-tiv)

. . . .

FUTILE
(FYOO-tuhl *or* FYOO-tahyl)

F

characterized by excess

*The **fulsome** celebration disgusted her; she would have preferred to enjoy her birthday quietly with family.*

Synonyms: excessive, extravagant, grandiloquent

· ·

done secretly or in an underhanded way

*They stole many **furtive** glances into the guarded room but saw nothing.*

Synonyms: cunning, sly, stealthy

· ·

useless

*Their efforts to build a dam were **futile**, and their home was completely flooded.*

Synonyms: hopeless, ineffective, pointless

GAINSAY

(GEYN-sey)

. . . .

GARRULOUS

(GAR-uh-luhs)

. . . .

GAUCHE

(gohsh)

G

to declare to be untrue

*You cannot **gainsay** the fact that though he has much more to learn, he has improved a great deal.*

Synonyms: contradict, deny, dispute, oppose

. . . .

talkative, generally in a rambling or annoying way

*I was hoping to rest during the flight, but unfortunately I was seated next to a **garrulous** young man.*

Synonyms: diffuse, verbose, wordy

. . . .

lacking good manners or tact, especially due to a lack of experience

*I am embarrassed to think how **gauche** it was for me to have brought up that sensitive topic in the middle of the dinner party.*

Synonyms: awkward, crude, insensitive, maladroit

GRE VOCABULARY

GENIAL
(JEE-nyuhl)

. . . .

GERMANE
(juhr-MEYN)

. . . .

GLIB
(glib)

friendly, sympathetic

His **genial** manners were the result of great effort, as he actually tended to be rather grouchy.

Synonyms: cheerful, cordial, easygoing, gracious, kind

. . . .

relevant, appropriate

Because your concerns are **germane** to the topic of the meeting, I would like to ask you to speak first.

Synonyms: applicable, connected, fitting, related

. . . .

informal, without thought or sincerity

His **glib** comment might have been insulting, except that everyone knew that he generally did not mean what he said.

Synonyms: flip, offhand, slick

GRE VOCABULARY

GOAD
(gohd)

. . . .

GRANDILOQUENCE
(gran-DI-luh-kwuhns)

. . . .

GREGARIOUS
(gri-GAR-ee-uhs)

to urge

*He might have quit years ago if his brother had not **goaded** him on.*

Synonyms: encourage, incite, stimulate

. . . .

lofty or extravagant manner, especially in speech

*The children giggled at the **grandiloquence** of the principal's speech on the first day of school; it would have been better for him to speak more simply.*

Synonyms: bombast, grandiosity, pomposity

. . . .

tending to be social

*A **gregarious** young woman, she held dinner parties at her home every Friday.*

Synonyms: convivial, friendly, outgoing

GUILELESS
(GAHYL-uhs)

. . . .

GUISE
(gahyz)

. . . .

GULLIBLE
(GUH-luh-buhl)

innocent, without deceit

*His phone call to his ex-girlfriend was truly **guileless**; he simply wanted to know whether or not she was well.*

Synonyms: honest, frank, sincere, straightforward

. . . .

appearance; style of dress

*The spy gained entry to the office in the **guise** of a job applicant.*

Synonyms: facade, posture, pretense

. . . .

easily duped

*I hope that you are not so **gullible** as to believe a single word of his tall tales.*

Synonyms: naive, trusting

HACKNEYED
(HAK-need)

....

HALCYON
(HAL-see-uhn)

....

HALLOWED
(HA-lohd)

lacking originality

*The critics panned the film because of its **hackneyed** boy-meets-girl plot.*

Synonyms: banal, cliche, stale, trite

· ·

calm, peaceful

*I love the **halcyon** days of mid-August, while we are still on vacation and before the mad rush of preparations for school begins.*

Synonyms: soothing, tranquil

· ·

holy, sacred

*The cemetery grounds are **hallowed** by those who are buried there.*

Synonyms: blessed, venerated

HARANGUE
(huh-RANG)

. . . .

HARROWING
(HAR-oh-ing)

. . . .

HEDONISM
(HEE-duh-ni-zuhm)

a rant

*We were taken aback by his bitter **harangue** against youth.*

Synonyms: diatribe, jeremiad, tirade

. . . .

extremely distressing or difficult

*Watching the horror movie was **harrowing** to her; she had no idea how her boyfriend could have enjoyed it.*

Synonyms: distressing, excruciating, grievous, terrifying

. . . .

devotion to pleasure, the doctrine that pleasure is the greatest good

*The **hedonism** of fraternity life enticed him.*

Synonyms: debauchery, indulgence

HEGEMONY
(hi-JE-muh-nee)

. . . .

HERETICAL
(huh-RE-ti-kuhl)

. . . .

HETERODOX
(HE-tuh-ruh-doks)

GRE VOCABULARY

[185]

pervasive influence or authority

*The cultural **hegemony** of the United States reaches every corner of the world.*

Synonyms: command, domination, power

. . . .

departing from accepted beliefs, characterized by heresy

*In the Middle Ages, it was dangerous to profess **heretical** beliefs.*

Synonyms: dissident, unorthodox

. . . .

contrary to an accepted standard, tradition, or belief, especially in religion

*She holds the **heterodox** view that the capacity for empathy evolved in humans before language did.*

Synonyms: dissident, unconventional, unorthodox

HOMOGENEOUS
(hoh-muh-JEE-nee-uhs *or*
hoh-muh-JEE-nyuhs)

. . . .

HUBRIS
(HYOO-bris)

. . . .

HYPERBOLE
(hahy-PUHR-buh-lee)

*It took some time for him to get used to the **homogeneous** population of his new home; he was accustomed to the diversity of the city.*

Synonyms: alike, consistent, uniform

. . . .

arrogance, pride

*It takes a certain amount of **hubris** to run for the office of the president of the United States.*

Synonyms: audacity, presumption, vanity

. . . .

composed of parts that are all alike; extravagant and intentional exaggeration

*His claim that it took him years to read the book was **hyperbole**; it actually took him only two weeks to finish.*

Synonyms: embellishment, hype, overstatement

ICONOCLAST
(ahy-KO-nuh-klast)

. . . .

IDOLATRY
(ahy-DO-luh-tree)

. . . .

IMBROGLIO
(im-BROHL-yoh)

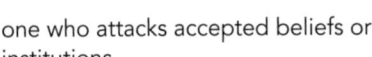

one who attacks accepted beliefs or institutions

*Charles Darwin delayed publication of the work introducing his theory of evolution for years, perhaps anticipating that he would be seen as an **iconoclast**.*

Synonyms: dissident, heretic, radical, rebel

. . . .

excessive or blind devotion

*Her devotion to the pop star bordered on **idolatry**; her bedroom was covered with images of him cut from magazines.*

Synonyms: adoration, adulation, fervor

. . . .

a complicated situation or painful misunderstanding, scandal

*The election devolved into an **imbroglio**, in which each side accused the other of fraud.*

Synonyms: brouhaha, dispute, quandary

IMMINENT
(I-muh-nuhnt)

. . . .

IMMUTABLE
(i-MYOO-tuh-buhl)

. . . .

IMPAIR
(im-PAIR)

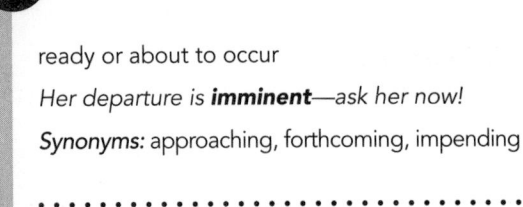

ready or about to occur

*Her departure is **imminent**—ask her now!*

Synonyms: approaching, forthcoming, impending

· ·

not subject to change

*They proclaimed their **immutable** devotion to each other in their wedding vows.*

Synonyms: constant, enduring, permanent, perpetual, unchangeable

· ·

to damage

*Better to wear the ugly safety goggles than to suffer an injury that could **impair** your vision.*

Synonyms: diminish, harm, hurt, injure

IMPASSIVE
(im-PA-siv)

. . . .

IMPECUNIOUS
(im-pi-KYU-nee-uhs)

. . . .

IMPEDE
(im-PEED)

not subject to pain, without feeling or emotion

*Though he seemed **impassive** at the collapse of his company, his wife could see that he was in despair.*

Synonyms: apathetic, dispassionate, stoic, unmoved

. . . .

having little or no money

*The **impecunious** poet believed he was far happier than the wealthiest businessperson.*

Synonyms: destitute, impoverished, penniless, poor

. . . .

to hinder, get in the way of

*An unexpected visit from friends from out of town **impeded** on her plan to paint the living room.*

Synonyms: hamper, interfere, obstruct

IMPERMEABLE
(im-PUHR-mee-uh-buhl)

. . . .

IMPERTURBABLE
(im-puhr-TUHR-buh-buhl)

. . . .

IMPERVIOUS
(im-PUHR-vee-uhs)

incapable of being penetrated or passed through

*The jacket is coated with a substance that renders it **impermeable** by water.*

Synonyms: impassable, impervious

. . . .

incapable of being disturbed

*By maintaining an **imperturbable** air through-out the crisis, she emerged as a steady and trustworthy leader.*

Synonyms: calm, composed, immovable, unexcited

. . . .

not allowing entrance, incapable of being harmed or disturbed

*He was **impervious** to criticism, which enabled him to experiment freely in his artwork.*

Synonyms: immune, resistant, unaffected

IMPETUOUS
(im-PE-chuh-wuhs)

. . . .

IMPLACABLE
(im-PLA-kuh-buhl)

. . . .

IMPLAUSIBLE
(im-PLAW-zi-buhl)

passionately impulsive

Her **impetuous** decision to go to Brazil took a moment to make, and transformed her life forever.

Synonyms: impassionate, spontaneous, unexpected

. . . .

impossible to appease

Although the team had been eliminated from contention in the playoffs, it proved to be an **implacable** opponent.

Synonyms: inflexible, merciless, relentless, uncompromising, unyielding

. . . .

unbelievable

He might have gotten away with the prank if his cover story had not been so **implausible**.

Synonyms: improbable, inconceivable, incredible, unreasonable

IMPLICIT
(im-PLI-suht)

. . . .

IMPLODE
(im-PLOHD)

. . . .

IMPUNITY
(im-PYOO-nuh-tee)

implied, existing as a potential within

Implicit in the many warnings that preceded their trip was the fact that their destination was a dangerous place.

Synonyms: understood, latent

. . . .

to violently collapse inward

*The building suddenly **imploded** under the weight of the snow.*

Synonyms: cave in, fold

. . . .

freedom from punishment or harm

*Because his father was the headmaster, he thought he could break the rules with **impunity**.*

Synonyms: freedom, license, privilege

INADVERTENT
(in-uhd-VUHR-tuhnt)

. . . .

INCHOATE
(in-KOH-uht)

. . . .

INCIPIENT
(in-SI-pee-uhnt)

unintentional, characterized by lack of thought or attention

*The error was both **inadvertent** and catastrophic.*

Synonyms: careless, negligent, thoughtless

. . . .

not yet developed, incompletely formed

*The first draft of her novel was an **inchoate** mess; with two years of revision she transformed it into a masterpiece.*

Synonyms: amorphous, formless, incoherent, rudimentary

. . . .

coming into being

*At this time, our travel plans are only **incipient**; check with us again next week and we will be able to tell you exactly where we are going and when.*

Synonyms: developing, inchoate, nascent

INCONGRUOUS
(in-KON-gruh-wuhs)

. . . .

INCONSEQUENTIAL
(in-kon-suh-KWEN-shuhl)

. . . .

INCORPORATE
(in-KOR-puh-reyt)

out of place, lacking harmony, inconsistent

*Her genius was such that she could compose a work for such **incongruous** instruments as a banjo and saxophone and have it sound not just beautiful, but inspired.*

Synonyms: conflicting, discordant, incompatible

. . . .

unimportant

*The paper was so brilliant that the few lapses in spelling and punctuation were **inconsequential**.*

Synonyms: insignificant, irrelevant, negligible, trivial

. . . .

to include, to unite in one body; to embody

*I will **incorporate** your ideas into the next draft of the plan.*

Synonyms: assimilate, combine, integrate

INDETERMINATE
(in-di-TUHR-muh-nuht)

. . . .

INDIFFERENT
(in-DI-fruhnt)

. . . .

INDIGENCE
(IN-di-juhnts)

not fixed or defined, vague

*The CEO was of an **indeterminate** age: she had gray hair and a lined face but spoke and moved with the energy of a teenager.*

Synonyms: indefinite, uncertain, undetermined, unsettled

. . . .

unbiased; not interested or concerned

***Indifferent** to the results of the election, many voters stayed home.*

Synonyms: detached, disinterested, unconcerned; apathetic

. . . .

complete poverty

*After losing what little they had in the earthquake, the villagers were left in a state of **indigence**.*

Synonyms: destitution, need, privation, want

INDOLENT
(IN-duh-luhnt)

. . . .

INERT
(i-NUHRT)

. . . .

INFELICITOUS
(in-fi-LI-suh-tuhs)

lazy

*He was accused of being **indolent** when in truth he lacked energy because of illness.*

Synonyms: idle, inactive, slothful, sluggish

. . . .

having no power to act or move

***Inert** and silent as rocks, the children sat and watched TV.*

Synonyms: dormant, inactive, motionless

. . . .

not appropriate, awkward

*Your joke about divorce was especially **infelicitous**, considering that our hostess and her husband have just separated.*

Synonyms: inapt, inappropriate, unfortunate, unsuitable

INGENUOUS
(in-JEN-yuh-wuhs)

. . . .

INHERENT
(in-HEHR-uhnt)

. . . .

INIMICAL
(i-NI-mi-kuhl)

characterized by childlike innocence or sincerity

*When she brought a bouquet of wildflowers to thank him, the **ingenuous** gesture won her his devotion.*

Synonyms: artless, candid, naive

. . . .

essential to the character or nature of

*Human babies have **inherent** needs to suckle and be held.*

Synonyms: characteristic, fundamental, intrinsic, innate

. . . .

hostile, like an enemy

*Poor hygiene is **inimical** to good health.*

Synonyms: adverse, opposed, unfriendly, unwelcoming

INNOCUOUS
(i-NO–kyuh-wuhs)

. . . .

INSENSIBLE
(in-SEN-suh-buhl)

. . . .

INSINUATE
(in-SIN-yuh-weyt)

harmless, unlikely to offend

*The dog looked fierce, but she was as **innocuous** as a gerbil.*

Synonyms: innocent, inoffensive, unobjectionable

. . . .

not able to feel or perceive; unaware

***Insensible** to the boredom of his students, the professor droned on and on.*

Synonyms: indifferent, oblivious, unconscious, unfeeling

. . . .

to introduce in a subtle or gradual way; to imply

*Do you mean to **insinuate** that it was I who took the cookies from the kitchen?*

Synonyms: allude, intimate, mention

INSIPID
(in-SI-puhd)

. . . .

INSULARITY
(in-syuh-LA-ruh-tee)

. . . .

INTANGIBLE
(in-TAN-juh-buhl)

lacking taste, dull

*He may have been a charming performer, but the music he played was **insipid** and full of clichés.*

Synonyms: banal, inane, vapid

. . . .

isolation; narrow-mindedness

*The **insularity** of her views was understand-able—if you considered just how little of the world she had seen.*

Synonyms: bigotry, parochialism, provinciality

. . . .

not tangible, incapable of being touched

*The things she loved best were **intangible**: sunny mornings and moonlit nights.*

Synonyms: immaterial, impalpable, incorporeal

INTERPOLATE
(in-TUHR-puh-leyt)

. . . .

INTIMATE
(IN-tuh-meyt)

. . . .

INTRACTABLE
(in-TRAK-tuh-buhl)

to add words into a conversation or text

*While listening to them discuss the movie, he couldn't help but **interpolate** with his enthusiasm for the acting.*

Synonyms: inject, insert, interject

. . . .

to communicate indirectly

*Did you mean to **intimate** that I do not deserve the job?*

Synonyms: hint, imply, suggest

. . . .

not easily managed, manipulated, or cured

*The child's difficulties in school had grown to seem **intractable**, but all it took to help her was a new teacher who encouraged her to read about topics that interested her.*

Synonyms: obstinate, stubborn

INTRANSIGENT
(in-TRAN-si-juhnt)

. . . .

INTROSPECTION
(in-truh-SPEK-shuhn)

. . . .

INTREPID
(in-TRE-puhd)

refusing to compromise

The congressman made a big show of being **intransigent** *on the issue of budget cuts, but quickly changed his position after seeing the results of the poll.*

Synonyms: inflexible, obstinate, resolute, stubborn, tenacious

. . . .

looking inward at one's own thoughts and feelings

Arlo generally spent the last hour of each day in quiet **introspection**, *sometimes listening to music and sometimes writing in his journal.*

Synonyms: contemplation, reflection

. . . .

courageous

The men who attempted to be the first to the South Pole were all **intrepid** *explorers, but not all of them were fortunate, and some died in the attempt.*

Synonyms: bold, brave, fearless

GRE VOCABULARY

INUNDATE
(I-nuhn-deyt)

. . . .

INURED
(i-NYOORD)

. . . .

INVECTIVE
(in-VEK-tiv)

I

to flood or overwhelm

*After her controversial speech, the mayor's office was **inundated** with letters, both pro and con.*

Synonyms: bury, drown, engulf, immerse, overflow, submerge

· ·

accustomed to difficulty or pain

*By the middle of January, we were **inured** to the darkness and cold of the northern winter.*

Synonyms: hardened, toughened

· ·

abusive language

*The **invective** she heaped on her colleague was completely out of proportion with the small error she had made.*

Synonyms: berating, diatribe, tirade

INVEIGH
(in-VEY)

. . . .

INVEIGLE
(in-VEY-guhl)

. . . .

INVETERATE
(in-VEH-tuh-ruht)

to protest or complain

*Several teachers wrote letters to the editor to **inveigh** against the proposed school budget cuts.*

Synonyms: admonish, denounce

. . . .

to win over or obtain

*The twins tried every trick in the book to **inveigle** permission from their parents to go to bed later.*

Synonyms: beguile, entice, manipulate, wheedle

. . . .

firmly established as a habit, practice, or feeling

*An **inveterate** gambler, he gradually lost everything he owned over the course of a decade.*

Synonyms: chronic, confirmed, entrenched, habitual

IRASCIBLE
(i-RA-suh-buhl)

. . . .

IRRESOLUTE
(i-RE-zuh-loot)

. . . .

ITINERANT
(ahy-TI-nuh-ruhnt)

having a hot temper, easily angered

*To our surprise, our **irascible** neighbor lightened up after he adopted a stray dog.*

Synonyms: cranky, fractious, grouchy, irritable, touchy

. . . .

not sure how to act

*Herman was **irresolute** in all things, from deciding what to eat for breakfast to choosing which college to attend.*

Synonyms: doubtful, hesitant, indecisive, tentative, uncertain, vacillating

. . . .

going from place to place

*The **itinerant** preacher usually passed through our town in August.*

Synonyms: nomadic, unsettled, vagrant, wandering

JAUNDICED
(JAWN-duhsd)

· ·

JOCOSE
(juh-KOHS)

· ·

JUGGERNAUT
(juh-guhr-NAWT)

showing or feeling resentment or hostility

*She walked around the gallery with a **jaundiced** air, bitter that her paintings were not among the work selected to be shown.*

Synonyms: bitter, envious

. . . .

tending to joke, characterized by joking

*Your **jocose** spirits have certainly brightened my day!*

Synonyms: humorous, jesting, merry, playful, witty

. . . .

a large and powerful movement or object that destroys anything in its path

*The radio personality became a political **juggernaut** that those in office had to reckon with.*

JUNTA
(HOON-tuh)

. . . .

JUXTAPOSE
(juhk-stuh-POHZ)

. . . .

a group ruling a country after having seized power, a council

*He was the only member of the **junta** who had not participated directly in the coup.*

Synonyms: assembly, faction

. . . .

to place together, side by side

*She liked to **juxtapose** contrasting images in her poems.*

Synonym: connect

KUDOS
(KOO-dohs)

. . . .

fame earned or praise given for an accomplishment

*Her colleagues gave her **kudos** for the well-deserved promotion.*

Synonyms: credit, esteem

LACONIC
(luh-KO-nik)

· ·

LAMBASTE
(lam-BAST)

· ·

LASCIVIOUS
(luh-SI-vee-uhs)

L

using few words

*His **laconic** replies of a sentence or two unfairly earned him a reputation for being rude.*

Synonyms: brusque, concise, succinct

. . . .

to attack violently or verbally

*In the days leading up to the game, she **lambasted** her opponent with a series of insults and threats.*

Synonyms: berate, censure

. . . .

given to lust; arousing desire

*Though they show nudes, these paintings are not intended to be **lascivious**.*

Synonyms: lewd, lustful, wanton

LASSITUDE
(LA-suh-tood)

· ·

LAUD
(lawd)

· ·

LETHARGIC
(luh-THAHR-jik)

L

a lack of energy, weariness

Her **lassitude** during the winter contrasted greatly with her energy and high spirits during the spring and summer.

Synonyms: fatigue, languor, lethargy, listlessness

· ·

to praise

At the award ceremony, the philanthropist was **lauded** for her generosity.

Synonyms: acclaim, celebrate, extol

· ·

drowsy, sluggish

We could not help but feel **lethargic** on that hot, humid, August afternoon.

Synonyms: indolent, lazy, listless

LEVEE
(LEH-vee)

· ·

LEVITY
(LEH-vi-tee)

· ·

LIBERAL
(LI-buh-ruhl)

an embankment designed to prevent flooding

The **levee** held back the river, even through the record-breaking rainfall.

Synonyms: bank, dam

. . . .

a lightness of character, attitude, or behavior

The professor's jokes brought some **levity** to his discussion of the otherwise dull topic.

Synonyms: buoyancy, frivolity

. . . .

characterized by generosity; not strict; tending to support political liberalism

As a philanthropist, he was **liberal**, often giving large gifts to his favorite causes.

Synonyms: altruistic, benevolent; progressive

LIBERTINE
(LI-buhr-teen)

. . . .

LIBIDO
(luh-BEE-doh)

. . . .

LITANY
(LI-tuh-nee)

a free thinker, one who is unbound by convention or morality

*Though she was a serious student, she was a **libertine** when it came to food and wine.*

Synonym: debauchee

. . . .

sexual drive

*He claimed that he had an uncontrollable **libido**, and could not therefore be expected to be faithful to just one girlfriend.*

Synonyms: lust, passion

. . . .

a lengthy account or recitation

*To visit Mrs. Earnshaw was to subject oneself to a **litany** of complaints about everything—from her long-dead husband to the neighbor's dog.*

Synonyms: catalogue, petition

LOG
(lawg)

. . . .

LOQUACIOUS
(loh-KWEY-shuhs)

. . . .

LUCID
(LOO-suhd)

L

the record of a voyage or of other events or activities

*They studied the captain's **log** in the hopes of discovering when and how the ship went astray.*

Synonyms: account, journal, register

. . . .

tending to or characterized by excessive talk

*Emily's **loquacious** roommate constantly distracted her from her studies.*

Synonyms: talkative, verbose, wordy

. . . .

full of light; clear to the understanding

*We were confident in our ability to complete the task after her **lucid** explanation of what needs to be done.*

Synonyms: bright, brilliant, radiant, shining; evident, intelligible, obvious

GRE VOCABULARY

LUMINOUS
(LOO-muh-nuhs)

. . . .

LUSTROUS
(LUHS-truhs)

. . . .

illuminated in or shining with light

*The full moon cast a **luminous** path of light across the ocean to the horizon.*

Synonyms: bright, brilliant, glowing, radiant, shining

. . . .

radiantly glowing

*We polished the floors until they took on a **lustrous** sheen.*

Synonyms: luminous, polished, shining

MACHIAVELLIAN
(ma-kee-uh-VEH-lee-uhn)

. . . .

MACHINATION
(ma-kuh-NEY-shun)

. . . .

MAGNANIMITY
(mag-nuh-NI-mi-tee)

characterized by cunning and duplicity

*Her plan to win the election was truly **Machiavellian**: she made many promises that she had no intention of keeping once she was in office.*

Synonyms: deceitful, devious, unscrupulous

. . . .

an artful or scheming act or design, which is aimed at an evil purpose

*All his **machinations** were aimed at framing her for the crime that he himself had committed.*

Synonyms: conspiracy, intrigue, strategem

. . . .

the possession of a courageous spirit and noble mind

*Her **magnanimity** was such that she never gossiped or even worried what others said about her.*

Synonyms: chivalry, generosity, philanthropy

MALEVOLENT
(muh-LE-vuh-luhnt)

. . . .

MALIGN
(muh-LAHYN)

. . . .

MALINGER
(muh-LING-guhr)

M

characterized by ill will or hatred

*His angry glare gave away his **malevolent** intentions.*

Synonyms: evil, hateful, vicious, vindictive

. . . .

to speak ill of, often falsely

*They **maligned** her academic record with false reports of her cheating.*

Synonyms: defame, misrepresent, slander

. . . .

to pretend illness in order to avoid an obligation or work

*His **malingering** cost him the friendships of many whom he had let down.*

Synonyms: dodge, evade, shirk

MALLEABLE
(MA-lee-uh-buhl)

· ·

MARTIAL
(MAHR-shuhl)

· ·

MAVERICK
(MAV-rik)

M

capable of being shaped or influenced

*Her opinions were so **malleable** that she tended to agree with whomever she had spoken to most recently.*

Synonyms: adaptable, pliable, supple, yielding

. . . .

having to do with war or military life

*His years in the Marines were apparent in his **martial** bearing.*

Synonyms: military, soldierly, warlike

. . . .

an independent or dissenting individual

*The senator's reputation for being a **maverick** was unearned; he tended to vote with his party.*

Synonyms: dissenter, nonconformist

MENAGERIE
(muh-NA-juh-ree)

. . . .

MENDACIOUS
(men-DEY-shuhs)

. . . .

MERCURIAL
(muhr-KYOOR-ee-uhl)

a collection of animals or the place where they are exhibited; a varied group of people

*Over the past century, this zoo has grown from the **menagerie** of its original benefactor to a great research institution.*

Synonyms: collection, exhibition

. . . .

dishonest

*Though the widely spread rumor of his affair was proven to be **mendacious**, it ruined his political career.*

Synonyms: deceitful, false, insincere

. . . .

characterized by quickly changing moods

*The toddler's **mercurial** temperament improved when he began to nap more regularly.*

Synonyms: changeable, erratic, fickle, flighty, unpredictable, volatile

GRE VOCABULARY

MESMERIZE
(MEZ-muh-rahyz)

....

METAMORPHOSIS
(me-tuh-MAWR-fuh-suhs)

....

METICULOUS
(muh-TI-kyuh-luhs)

to hypnotize

*The music **mesmerized** us with its repetitive, pulsing sounds.*

Synonym: spellbind

. . . .

a change in physical form, substance, or character, often through supernatural means

*The summertime seemed to work a **metamorphosis** on her, as all her anxiety about her schoolwork was lifted.*

Synonyms: mutation, rebirth, transformation

. . . .

taking care of details

*Her **meticulous** approach to language served her well in her work as an editor.*

Synonyms: exacting, finicky, fussy, painstaking, scrupulous, thorough

METTLE
(ME-tuhl)

. . . .

MILITATE
(MI-luh-teyt)

. . . .

MINUSCULE
(mi-nuh-SKYOOL)

strength of spirit or temperament

*She showed her **mettle** by completing the marathon.*

Synonyms: courage, fortitude, stamina

• •

to work against or fight

*Though the issue was settled, they continued to **militate** against the mayor's choice for a deputy.*

• •

tiny

*The type was so **miniscule** that she needed a magnifying glass to read it.*

Synonyms: little, miniature, minute

MISANTHROPE
(MI-suhn-throhp)

· ·

MISCELLANY
(mi-suh-LEY-nee)

· ·

MISOGYNIST
(mi-SO-juh-nist)

M

one who tends to dislike or distrust humanity

*The hermit was a **misanthrope** who preferred the company of trees to that of humans.*

Synonyms: cynic, skeptic

• •

a collection of different writings; a varied group

*The small volume was a **miscellany** of journal entries, haiku, and to-do lists.*

Synonyms: assortment, hodgepodge

• •

one who hates women

*He was a **misogynist** who tried to pay female employees less than their male counterparts.*

MITIGATE
(MI-tuh-geyt)

. . . .

MNEMONIC
(ni-MO-nik)

. . . .

MOLLIFY
(MO-luh-fahy)

to make less hostile or severe

*Though she knew that her phobia was irrational, little could be done to **mitigate** her fear of even the most harmless snakes.*

Synonyms: allay, alleviate, assuage, ease, moderate, mollify

. . . .

(*adj.*) helping the memory, related to memory

*Acronyms like PEMDAS can be useful **mnemonic** devices.*

(*n.*) something that aids the memory

*I use the **mnemonic** PEMDAS to help me remember the order of operations: parentheses, exponents, multiplication and division, and addition and subtraction.*

Synonyms: cue, hint, prompt, reminder

. . . .

to soften the temper or feeling

*The children's sincere apology **mollified** their offended neighbor.*

Synonyms: appease, mellow, mitigate, pacify, placate

MONOLITHIC
(mo-nuh-LI-thik)

. . . .

MOROSE
(muh-ROHS)

. . . .

MUNDANE
(muhn-DEYN)

huge, forming one giant whole

*The **monolithic** statues on Easter Island are haunting and mysterious.*

Synonyms: colossal, enormous, massive

. . . .

gloomy or sullen in mood or temperament

*Hating the fact that he was only getting older, he was especially **morose** on his birthday.*

Synonyms: dour, melancholy, pessimistic

. . . .

earthly, practical, ordinary

*The philosopher could speak brilliantly and at length about the most abstract ideas, but had trouble taking care of such **mundane** matters as washing the dishes and paying the bills.*

Synonyms: banal, common, everyday, prosaic, unimaginative

NASCENT
(NEY-suhnt)

. . . .

NEBULOUS
(NE-byuh-luhs)

. . . .

NEGATE
(ni-GEYT)

just coming into existence

*The crocuses were the first sign of the **nascent** spring.*

Synonyms: burgeoning, fledgling, incipient

. . . .

vague

*He had only **nebulous** ideas of what type of profession he might like to pursue.*

Synonyms: confused, hazy, indefinite, indistinct, unclear

. . . .

to deny the truth or existence of; to make ineffective

*The teacher's feedback is intended to help you improve your writing, and should not be seen as **negating** your effort or accomplishments.*

Synonyms: annul, cancel, contradict, invalidate, nullify, refute

NEOLOGISM
(nee-O-luh-ji-zuhm)

. . . .

NEOPHYTE
(NEE-uh-fahyt)

. . . .

NOSTALGIA
(nuh-STAL-juh)

a new word

The rapid development of technology in recent years has required the creation of many **neologisms***.*

Synonym: coinage

. . . .

a beginner or new convert

Though he claimed to be an expert, he made the mistakes of a **neophyte***.*

Synonyms: novice, recruit, rookie

. . . .

a state of longing for the past

I always feel such **nostalgia** *for my childhood home when I smell the scent of baking bread.*

Synonyms: homesickness, longing, yearning

NOXIOUS
(NOK-shuhs)

. . . .

poisonous or corrupting

*The burning garbage emitted **noxious** fumes.*

Synonyms: deadly, injurious, harmful, pernicious, toxic

OBDURATE
(OB-duh-ruht)

. . . .

OBFUSCATE
(OB-fuh-skeyt)

. . . .

OBSEQUIOUS
(uhb-SEE-kwee-uhs)

unyielding to persuasion or softening feelings; persistent in doing wrong

*Though the evidence showed otherwise, he was **obdurate** in his belief that his employees were stealing from the till.*

Synonyms: implacable, inflexible, obstinate, stubborn

· ·

to confuse or make obscure

*The more information he gave us in an attempt to clarify what he was saying, the more he actually **obfuscated** his meaning.*

Synonyms: baffle, bewilder, conceal, perplex

· ·

characterized by fawning or servile attentiveness

*Your **obsequious** behavior is not going to earn you any favors from the teacher; it would be better simply to attend to your studies.*

Synonyms: deferential, groveling, submissive, subservient

OBSTINATE
(OB-stuh-nuht)

. . . .

OBTUSE
(ob-TOOS)

. . . .

OBVIATE
(OB-vee-eyt)

persistent in a belief or behavior; not easily remedied, changed, or controlled

*The **obstinate** toddler refused to wear shoes.*

Synonyms: determined, dogged, stubborn, unyielding

. . . .

lacking quickness or insight in perception or intelligence

*I apologize for being so **obtuse**, but could you please explain the procedure one more time?*

Synonyms: dense, dull, imperceptive, stupid

. . . .

to prevent or make unnecessary through anticipation

*Our careful preparations for the move **obviated** the expense of having the movers help us pack.*

Synonyms: avert, hinder, preclude

OCCLUDE
(uh-KLOOD)

. . . .

ODIOUS
(OH-dee-uhs)

. . . .

OFFICIOUS
(uh-FI-shuhs)

to block off or conceal

A lunar eclipse results when the Moon **occludes** *the light from the Sun.*

Synonyms: hinder, impede, obstruct

• •

causing or deserving of hatred

After they were found guilty of vandalism, the teens were punished for their **odious** *behavior.*

Synonyms: detestable, disgusting, loathsome, offensive, repugnant

• •

giving service where none was asked for

Her **officious** *contributions to the project were more a hindrance than a help, and we ended up having to redo much of what she had done.*

Synonyms: intrusive, meddlesome, pushy

GRE VOCABULARY

ONEROUS
(OH-nuhr-uhs)

· ·

OPAQUE
(oh-PEYK)

· ·

OPPROBRIUM
(uh-PRO-bree-uhm)

burdensome

*The homework proved to be far less **onerous** than we had expected, and we finished it all in less than an hour.*

Synonyms: arduous, oppressive, troublesome

. . . .

blocking light, dark; difficult to understand

*The reading assignment was only eight pages long, but the text was so **opaque** that it took me two hours to read it.*

Synonyms: cloudy, impenetrable, murky; concealed, incomprehensible, obscure, unclear

. . . .

public disgrace or something that causes disgrace

*Fearing the **opprobrium** that would result if his secrets were revealed, he quietly left town, never to return.*

Synonyms: dishonor, disrepute, infamy

OSCILLATE
(O-suh-leyt)

. . . .

OSTENTATIOUS
(os-tuhn-TEY-shuhs)

. . . .

to swing back and forth; to vary in opinions, beliefs, or conditions

*After her busy week was over, she found herself **oscillating** between a fierce desire to go out dancing and a just as fierce desire to snuggle up in bed.*

Synonyms: fluctuate, vacillate

. . . .

characterized by showy or pretentious display

*Her philanthropy always struck me as **ostentatious**: done to impress others rather than for the purpose of giving itself.*

Synonyms: conspicuous, extravagant, flamboyant, flashy

PAEAN
(PEE-uhn)

· ·

PALLID
(PA-luhd)

· ·

PARAGON
(PAR-uh-gon)

P

a song of praise, thanksgiving, or triumph

*Beethoven's "Ode to Joy" is a **paean** to the kinship of all humanity.*

Synonyms: anthem, hymn, laud, ode

. . . .

lacking color or energy

*Brad claimed that he felt just fine, but his **pallid** skin indicated otherwise.*

Synonyms: dull, pale, wan

. . . .

an example of excellence

*As a student, Gina was thought to be a **paragon**, but her English teacher noticed that she excelled only because she refused to take any risks.*

Synonyms: epitome, exemplar, nonpareil, standard

PARODY
(PAR-roh-dee)

. . . .

PARTISAN
(PAHR-tuh-zuhn)

. . . .

PATHOLOGICAL
(pa-thuh-LO-ji-kuhl)

P

a work of literature, music, theater, or film that imitates the style of another, for humorous or satirical effect

*The seniors performed a **parody** of Hamlet that had us all in stiches.*

Synonyms: caricature, spoof

. . . .

committed to or biased toward a party, cause, or person

*It seems that **partisan** politics are getting in the way of the ability of Congress to get anything done.*

Synonyms: factional, partial, prejudiced

. . . .

caused by or symptomatic of disease or mental disturbance

*His dread of travel was so extreme as to seem **pathological**.*

PAUCITY
(PAW-suh-tee)

. . . .

PEDAGOGY
(PEH-duh-goh-jee)

. . . .

PEDANTIC
(pi-DAN-tik)

P

scarcity

*The **paucity** of information about the region has led many myths to take hold about it and those who live there.*

Synonyms: dearth, deficiency, lack

. . . .

the art or science of teaching

*A successful teacher needs both a thorough grounding in his or her subject area and a solid understanding of **pedagogy**.*

Synonyms: education, study

. . . .

ostentatious and unimaginative in one's learning

*You might excite more of your students if your approach to your subject were less **pedantic**.*

Synonyms: academic, didactic, scholastic

PENCHANT
(PEN-chuhnt)

. . . .

PENURY
(PEN-yuh-ree)

. . . .

PEREMPTORY
(puh-REMP-tuh-ree)

P

a strong inclination

With her **penchant** *for working with her hands, she is likely to enjoy her new job at the botanic garden.*

Synonyms: fondness, liking, tendency

. . . .

extreme poverty

He spent his childhood in a state of such **penury** *that it affected his health for the rest of his life.*

Synonyms: dearth, destitution, indigence, scarcity

. . . .

allowing of no contradiction; characterized by arrogance

After his promotion, his **peremptory** *attitude toward his former colleagues alienated them from him.*

Synonyms: imperative, unconditional; dictatorial, imperious

PERENNIAL
(puh-RE-nee-uhl)

. . . .

PERFIDY
(PUHR-fuh-dee)

. . . .

PERFUNCTORY
(puhr-FUHNGK-tuh-ree)

P

lasting a long time, persistent, constant

*Their **perennial** complaint was that management did not budget sufficient resources for them to do their work properly.*

Synonyms: continuing, everlasting, perpetual, recurrent

· ·

an act of disloyalty, treachery

*His scoring a touchdown for the opposing team was not an act of **perfidy** so much as a stupid mistake.*

Synonyms: betrayal, duplicity, infidelity

· ·

done in a routine, superficial, or indifferent way

*Maggie's **perfunctory** greeting indicated that we were not the visitors she was hoping to see.*

Synonyms: automatic, mechanical, offhand, unthinking

PERMEABLE
(PUHR-mee-uh-buhl)

. . . .

PERNICIOUS
(puhr-NI-shuhs)

. . . .

PERSPICACIOUS
(puhr-spuh-KAY-shuhs)

P

able to be **permeated** or penetrated

We cannot use this fabric to make a tent because it is permeable to water.

Synonyms: absorbent, penetrable, porous

· ·

destructive or deadly

*These **pernicious** lies could ruin more than just your career.*

Synonyms: detrimental, harmful, injurious, noxious, ruinous

· ·

extremely perceptive

*The **perspicacious** child knew long before he was told that his mother was pregnant again.*

Synonyms: discerning, intelligent, keen, shrewd

PERTURB
(puhr-TUHRB)

. . . .

PERUSE
(puh-ROOZ)

. . . .

PERVADE
(puhr-VEYD)

P

to disturb mentally

*I was so **perturbed** by that movie that I had nightmares every night for more than a week afterward.*

Synonyms: agitate, derange, trouble, unsettle, upset

. . . .

to study with attention to detail; to look over casually

*Please **peruse** the report carefully before the meeting.*

Synonyms: analyze, examine, inspect; browse, scan, skim

. . . .

to become spread throughout

*The scent of his heavy cologne **pervaded** every corner of the office.*

Synonyms: diffuse, infuse, permeate

PETULANT
(PE-chuh-luhnt)

. . . .

PHLEGMATIC
(fleg-MA-tik)

. . . .

PIOUS
(PAHY-uhs)

characterized by rudeness or ill humor

*The **petulant** child just needed some rest; after her nap, she was perfectly cheerful.*

Synonyms: crabby, fractious, grouchy, irritable, moody

. . . .

having an unexcitable or sluggish temperament

*The brothers could not have been any more different: whereas Tom was loud and quick tempered, Tim was **phlegmatic**.*

Synonyms: apathetic, dispassionate, indifferent, lethargic, unemotional

. . . .

characterized by religious devotion or by conspicuous and hypocritical virtue

*Our **pious** neighbor goes to church every day.*

Synonyms: devout, religious, reverent, righteous, sanctimonious, scrupulous

GRE VOCABULARY

PINE
(payhn)

. . . .

PIRATE
(PAHY-ruht)

. . . .

PITHY
(PI-thee)

P

to long painfully, often for something unattainable; to waste away from grief

*The new father **pined** for his family through his first day back to work after the birth of his child.*

Synonyms: grieve, yearn

. . . .

to take or reproduce without the right to do so

*We did not **pirate** the recordings; the band gave us permission to distribute their work.*

Synonyms: copy, plagiarize, steal

. . . .

brief and meaningful

*Benjamin Franklin's proverbs are **pithy** statements about living well.*

Synonyms: cogent, expressive, pointed, succinct, terse

PLACATE
(PLEY-keyt)

. . . .

PLAINTIVE
(PLEYN-tiv)

. . . .

PLASTICITY
(pla-STI-suh-tee)

to calm or pacify, especially by giving concessions

To **placate** the disappointed children, the teacher promised that the outing would be rescheduled for a time after the rain cleared.

Synonyms: appease, assuage, conciliate, mollify, soothe

· ·

expressing sorrow

The **plaintive** call of the loon seemed to be telling of our own sadness on the morning we left the lake for good.

Synonyms: melancholy, mournful

· ·

the capacity to be changed or molded

The play dough lost much of its **plasticity** after just one day, and the following day it was as hard as a rock.

Synonyms: malleability, pliancy

· ·

PLATITUDE
(PLA-tuh-tood)

. . . .

PLETHORA
(PLE-thuh-ruh)

. . . .

PLUMMET
(PLUH-muht)

P

a banal or trite statement

*The fortune teller studied my palm and then uttered a series of **platitudes** that could be true for just about anyone.*

Synonym: commonplace

. . . .

an excess or abundance of

*The **plethora** of fruits and vegetables at the farmers' market overwhelmed us; we had no idea what to choose.*

Synonyms: glut, surplus

. . . .

to fall or drop sharply and suddenly

*In her terror of heights, she kept imagining herself **plummeting** from the edge of the loft, even though a barrier made it nearly impossible to fall off.*

Synonyms: collapse, plunge

POLEMICAL
(puh-LEM-i-kuhl)

. . . .

POROUS
(POHR-uhs)

. . . .

PRAGMATIC
(prag-MA-tik)

P

controversial; tending toward disputes or controversy

*Though the essay was not intended to be **polemical**, it inspired many angry letters to the editor of the publication.*

Synonyms: argumentative, contentious

. . . .

having pores, permeable to fluids

*Some rocks, like pumice, are actually **porous** and can absorb water.*

Synonyms: absorbent, penetrable

. . . .

oriented toward the practical

*Our **pragmatic** mother preferred to receive useful gifts for her birthday.*

Synonyms: businesslike, efficient, utilitarian

PRATTLE
(PRA-tuhl)

. . . .

PRECARIOUS
(pri-KER-ee-uhs)

. . . .

PRECIPITATE
(pri-SI-puh-teyt)

chatter or babble

*The **prattle** and laughter of her students filled Ms. Shapiro's classroom.*

Synonym: idle talk

. . . .

dependent on uncertain or chance circumstances

*Her position at the company felt increasingly **precarious** as more and more of her colleagues were let go.*

Synonyms: contingent, insecure, perilous, shaky, unreliable

. . . .

to cause, to bring about in a rushed or sudden way; to come out of solution

*His idle remark **precipitated** an argument between his parents*

Synonyms: hasten, hurry, speed

PRECURSOR
(pri-KUHR-suhr)

. . . .

PREDILECTION
(pre-duh-LEK-shuhn)

. . . .

PREEN
(preen)

that which precedes or anticipates another

*Athenian democracy is regarded as a **precursor** to ours, although it functioned very differently than any democracy does today.*

Synonyms: forerunner, predecessor

. . . .

a preference for something

*The boss's **predilection** for loud jazz music was barely tolerable to anyone he worked with.*

Synonyms: bias, inclination, penchant, tendency

. . . .

to groom, to dress smartly; to congratulate oneself for an accomplishment

*You may **preen** yourself until you look as glamorous as can be, but if you behave rudely, you will not impress.*

Synonym: primp

PREMONITION
(pre-muh-NI-shuhn)

. . . .

PRESCIENCE
(PRE-shuhns)

. . . .

PRESUMPTUOUS
(pri-ZUHMP-choo-uhs)

a sense of anticipation of a future event

*Her **premonition** of failure had everything to do with her anxiety and little to do with reason.*

Synonyms: forewarning, presentiment

• •

foresight, through either divine means or normal human anticipation

*Even though the day began without a cloud in the sky, he had the **prescience** to bring rain gear.*

Synonym: foreknowledge

• •

overstepping bounds, such as of courtesy

*May I be so **presumptuous** as to suggest that you repaint your living room walls?*

Synonyms: audacious, bold, overconfident

PREVARICATE
(pri-VAR-uh-keyt)

. . . .

PRISTINE
(pris-TEEN)

. . . .

PROBITY
(PROH-buh-tee)

P

to lie

*Do not **prevaricate** about who did what or why; simply tell me how the vase got broken.*

Synonyms: deceive, equivocate, misrepresent

. . . .

fresh, unspoiled, clean

*She gazed at the **pristine** canvas, enjoying the possibilities it offered while still untouched by her paints.*

Synonyms: immaculate, pure

. . . .

maintenance of virtue and honesty

*In To Kill a Mockingbird, the **probity** of Atticus Finch is such that he is the same man in his living room as out on the street.*

Synonyms: fidelity, integrity, sincerity, uprightness

PROBLEMATIC
(prob-luh-MA-tik)

. . . .

PROCLIVITY
(proh-KLI-vuh-tee)

. . . .

PRODIGAL
(PRO-di-guhl)

posing a problem, unsettled

Your claim is **problematic**, *insofar as it does not apply to those who earn below the median household income.*

Synonyms: doubtful, questionable, uncertain

· ·

tendency

Her **proclivity** *toward fussy tidiness was severely challenged when her baby became a spirited and messy toddler.*

Synonyms: inclination, predilection, propensity

· ·

characterized by lavish, wasteful, or reckless expense; abundant

Nature is **prodigal** *in its resources; unfortunately, humanity is prodigal in using those resources.*

Synonyms: excessive, extravagant; bountiful

GRE VOCABULARY

PRODIGIOUS
(pruh-DI-juhs)

. . . .

PROFLIGATE
(PRO-fli-guht)

. . . .

PROFUSE
(pruh-FYOOS)

inspiring wonder; extraordinary in size or degree

*They celebrated the grand wedding with a **prodigious** feast.*

Synonyms: exceptional, extraordinary, fabulous, marvelous; huge, enormous

• •

given to dissipation or extravagance

*After your **profligate** behavior all semester long, how could you expect anything but the poorest grades?*

Synonyms: corrupt, immoral, licentious, shameless, wanton

• •

abundant without restraint

*Their **profuse** compliments were as unexpected as they were welcome.*

Synonyms: excessive, generous, liberal, plentiful

PROLIFIC
(pruh-LI-fik)

. . . .

PROPENSITY
(pruh-PEN-suh-tee)

. . . .

PROPITIATE
(proh-PI-shee-eyt)

P

abundantly productive, fertile

*She is not only a talented writer, but **prolific**, completing one or two novels every year.*

Synonyms: bountiful, fruitful, teeming

. . . .

a natural tendency or preference

*I have a **propensity** to eat too much when I am nervous.*

Synonyms: inclination, predilection, proclivity

. . . .

to gain or regain the favor of

*To **propitiate** her boss, she began to bring him snacks and coffee in the afternoon.*

Synonyms: appease, conciliate

PROPRIETY
(pruh-PRAHY-uh-tee)

....

PROSAIC
(proh-ZEY-ik)

....

PROSCRIBE
(pro-SKRAHYB)

P

the state of being proper or appropriate

Propriety in speech was so important to him that even in his most heated moments he never used harsh language.

Synonyms: appropriateness, correctness, decorum, respectability

• •

dull, factual

*She once had romantic visions of life as the editor of a literary magazine; the reality was **prosaic**, involving demanding production schedules and temperamental writers.*

Synonyms: commonplace, unimaginative

• •

to forbid

*After the accident, all alcoholic beverages were **proscribed** from the stadium.*

Synonyms: banish, condemn, outlaw, prohibit

PUNGENT
(PUHN-juhnt)

. . . .

PURPORT
(puhr-POHRT)

. . . .

PUTREFY
(PYOO-truh-fahy)

P

sharp, painful, to the point

*The rejection was brief and **pungent**.*

Synonyms: acrid, biting, caustic

. . . .

to claim or pretend

*This manuscript **purports** to be the original, but it looks like a copy to me.*

Synonyms: allege, assert

. . . .

to rot

*The fruit that fell from the trees began to **putrefy** within a day or two.*

Synonyms: decay, spoil, stink

QUAFF
(kwof)

. . . .

QUAGMIRE
(KWAG-mahyr)

. . . .

QUALIFIED
(KWO-luh-feyd)

Q

to drink deeply with great enjoyment

*We shall raise our glasses high in a toast and then **quaff** our ale in celebration!*

Synonyms: down, imbibe

· ·

soft land that gives underfoot; a difficult situation

*The couple was sinking in a **quagmire** of debt.*

Synonyms: bog; predicament, quandary

· ·

to be suitable for a particular purpose; modified or restricted in some way

*Her acceptance of our invitation was **qualified**: she could come only if she could find a ride home.*

Synonyms: capable, competent, proper, skillful; conditional, contingent

QUALM
(kwom)

. . . .

QUERY
(KWEER-ee)

. . . .

QUERULOUS
(KWER-uh-luhs)

a feeling of apprehension or uneasiness, often for reasons of conscience or propriety

*He had many **qualms** about living on the other side of the country from his aging parents.*

Synonyms: apprehension, misgiving, uncertainty

. . . .

question

*Your lengthy explanation certainly answered my **query**, and more!*

Synonym: inquiry

. . . .

given to complaining

*Few of his classmates liked the **querulous** child, which only made him more irritable.*

Synonyms: dissatisfied, fretful, whining

QUIBBLE
(KWI-buhl)

· ·

QUIESCENT
(kwayh-EH-suhnt)

· ·

QUIXOTIC
(kwik-SAH-tik)

to evade a point through ambiguous or irrelevant arguments

*They **quibbled** over the details so long that
they went over budget and failed to meet their
deadline.*

Synonyms: bicker, equivocate

. . . .

at rest, latent

*My mind is hardly **quiescent** in sleep: my
dreams are busy, sometimes even panicked.*

Synonyms: dormant, inactive, motionless,
quiet, still

. . . .

extravagantly foolish or romantic in the pursuit
of ideals

*I am not so **quixotic** to think that my leader-
ship can transform this school in just one year,
but I do believe that I can make a difference.*

Synonyms: chivalrous, impractical, visionary

QUOTIDIAN
(kwoh-TI-dee-uhn)

....

ordinary

After our arduous journey, it was good to return to our **quotidian** *concerns: getting the children to school and ourselves to work.*

Synonyms: commonplace, daily, everyday, usual

RANCOROUS
(RANG-kuh-ruhs)

....

RAREFIED
(RER-uh-fahyd)

....

RATIONALE
(ra-shuh-NAL)

characterized by deep ill will

*Over the course of a few days, their argument became so **rancorous** that reconciliation seemed impossible.*

Synonyms: bitter, virulent

• •

elevated; related to or appealing to a small, elite group

*Vivian does not share her parents' **rarefied** taste for the work of minimalist composers; she prefers rock 'n' roll.*

Synonyms: esoteric, lofty, select

• •

the basis of an opinion or belief

*Her **rationale** for stealing towels from hotels was that everyone else does it too.*

Synonyms: explanation, justification, reason

GRE VOCABULARY

RECALCITRANT
(ri-KAL-suh-truhnt)

. . . .

RECANT
(ri-KANT)

. . . .

RECLUSE
(REH-kloos)

stubbornly defiant, unmanageable, resistant

The class of third-grade students proved to be **recalcitrant** *to all the demands of the inexperienced substitute teacher.*

Synonyms: disobedient, intractable, uncontrollable

. . . .

to openly and formally withdraw or disavow a statement or belief

Regrettable as they were, she refused to **recant** *the rash statements she had made the night before.*

Synonyms: nullify, retract, void

. . . .

one who has withdrawn from society

We rarely see my brother, a **recluse** *who lives in the woods with only his dog.*

Synonym: hermit

RECONDITE
(RE-kuhn-dahyt)

. . . .

REDOUBTABLE
(ri-DOU-tuh-buhl)

. . . .

REFRACTORY
(ri-FRAK-tuh-ree)

GRE VOCABULARY

R

hidden, difficult to understand

*Her book dealt with such **recondite** matters as Kantian ethics.*

Synonyms: esoteric, mysterious, obscure, profound

. . . .

inspiring fear or respect

*He is a **redoubtable** scholar whose works are as entertaining as they are impressive.*

Synonyms: awesome, eminent, formidable, illustrious

. . . .

resistant to authority; resistant to treatment

*As **refractory** as a mule, he never earned his diploma because he refused to complete the necessary battery of tests.*

Synonyms: disobedient, rebellious, uncontrollable, unyielding

REFULGENT
(ri-FUHL-juhnt)

. . . .

REFUTE
(ri-FYOOT)

. . . .

RELEGATE
(RE-luh-geyt)

shining brightly

*Even from a distance, the **refulgent** city seemed to light up the sky.*

Synonyms: brilliant, gleaming, radiant

. . . .

to prove wrong, to deny

*He could not **refute** the evidence against him, and in the end, he confessed to the crime.*

Synonyms: disprove, invalidate, repudiate

. . . .

to banish, to assign to an insignificant or inferior place or role

*After the offices were renovated, we were **relegated** to a central room with no windows.*

Synonyms: demote, displace

RENEGE
(ri-NEG)

. . . .

REPARATION
(re-puh-REY-shuhn)

. . . .

REPROACH
(ri-PROHCH)

to go back on a commitment

*Karen **reneged** on her promise to come out with us only because of illness.*

Synonym: default

. . . .

making amends for damages or a wrong

*In **reparation** for years of neglect, the town finally invested an unprecedented amount in the schools, streets, and park in its poorest neighborhood.*

Synonyms: atonement, compensation, satisfaction

. . . .

(n.) an expression of disapproval or the act of expressing disapproval

*The teacher's **reproaches** fell on deaf ears, and the students continued to chatter while working on their writing.*

Synonyms: criticism, rebuke

(v.) to express disapproval

*Trevor's mother **reproached** him for failing to write a thank-you note to his grandmother.*

Synonyms: admonish, criticize, disparage a depraved person

GRE VOCABULARY

REPROBATE
(RE-pruh-beyt)

. . . .

REPUDIATE
(ri-PYOO-dee-eyt)

. . . .

RESCIND
(ri-SIND)

R

He was a **reprobate** who occasionally even stole cash from his elderly mother's purse.

pariah, fiend, miscreant

. . . .

to disown or reject

*Consider your words carefully before you decide to publicly **repudiate** the claims made by your boss.*

Synonyms: condemn, disown, renounce

. . . .

to take away or cancel

*She could not **rescind** the order she had mistakenly made for a bridesmaid dress in the wrong color.*

Synonyms: annul, invalidate, retract, revoke

RETICENT
(RE-tuh-suhnt)

. . . .

REVERENCE
(REV-ruhnts)

. . . .

RHETORIC
(RE-tuh-rik)

tending to be uncommunicative or silent

*Thinking her parents would not approve, Hannah was **reticent** about her plans to move to Brazil.*

Synonyms: reserved, restrained

. . . .

feelings of honor or respect

*Bruce treated the baseball with **reverence** after his favorite pitcher signed it.*

Synonyms: awe, deference, veneration

. . . .

the study or art of the use of language in speech or writing

*The electorate did not care for his highfalutin **rhetoric** and voted him out of office after just one term.*

RUE
(roo)

· ·

RUSE
(rooz)

· ·

discourse

to feel regret or sorrow, to wish that something had never been

*I **rue** the day that I first took up this game: I've found it to be completely addictive!*

Synonyms: deplore, grieve, mourn, regret

. . . .

a trick

*What he could not get directly through hard work, he decided to acquire indirectly through a **ruse**.*

Synonyms: artifice, deceit, stratagem, subterfuge

SAGE
(seyj)

· ·

SALUBRIOUS
(suh-LOO-bree-uhs)

· ·

SANCTION
(SANGK-shuhn)

one who is wise

*They treated me as a **sage** simply for having worked there longer than anyone else.*

Synonyms: guru, master

. . . .

healthful

*This purportedly **salubrious** drink is actually hardly more than sugar water.*

Synonyms: beneficial, wholesome

. . . .

to approve, give permission

*I cannot believe that your parents would **sanction** such rude behavior.*

Synonyms: allow, authorize, endorse

SARDONIC
(sahr-DON-ik)

. . . .

SATIATE
(SEY-shee-eyt)

. . . .

SATIRE
(SA-tahyr)

disdainfully or skeptically humorous or mocking

Joseph's **sardonic** *attitude toward his parents' interests was somewhat insulting, but also expected from a teenager.*

Synonyms: cynical, scornful, sneering

. . . .

to satisfy fully or supply to excess

This Thanksgiving dinner will surely **satiate** *even the hungriest of us all!*

Synonyms: fill, gratify, indulge

. . . .

the use of irony or ridicule to expose human folly

The novel is meant to be a **satire***; the author is ridiculing the views of the characters, not endorsing them.*

Synonyms: irony, mockery, parody

SATURATE
(SA-chuh-reyt)

. . . .

SAVOR
(SEY-vuhr)

. . . .

SECRETE
(si-KREET)

to fill completely or infuse with something until nothing more can be absorbed

*The air in and around the garden was **saturated** with the scent of lilacs.*

Synonyms: drench, soak

. . . .

to taste or smell with pleasure, enjoy

*I eat lobster once every year, while I'm on vacation, and I **savor** it each time.*

Synonyms: appreciate, relish

. . . .

to give off or release a substance or secretion such as sweat; to hide

*The tree **secreted** a sticky sap from the area of the trunk that was injured.*

Synonyms: discharge, emit; conceal

SEDULOUS
(SE-juh-luhs)

. . . .

SENSUAL
(SEN-shuh-wuhl)

. . . .

SENSUOUS
(SEN-shuh-wuhs)

characterized or produced by perseverance

*Through **sedulous** effort, Karen mastered conversational French in just six months.*

Synonyms: diligent, industrious, tireless

. . . .

related to the senses, especially with the gratification of or indulgence in the senses or appetites

*Their interest in each other was purely **sensual**, and so their relationship was passionate but brief.*

Synonyms: carnal, materialistic

. . . .

affecting the senses, aesthetically gratifying to the senses

*The singer was beloved for her **sensuous** style.*

Synonyms: luxurious, pleasurable

SENTIENT
(SEN-shee-uhnt)

· ·

SERVILE
(SUHR-vahyl)

· ·

SHARD
(shahrd)

conscious, able to perceive

*The forest seemed to be haunted, as though the trees were **sentient**.*

Synonym: aware

. . . .

submissive, like a slave

*Though yours is the lowest position in the firm, there is no need to behave in such a **servile** way, especially if you hope to be promoted.*

Synonyms: abject, obedient, subservient

. . . .

a fragment of a hard or brittle substance

*After he glued together the **shards** of the broken vase, the resulting vessel was off-kilter and oddly beautiful.*

Synonym: scrap

SINGULAR
(SING-gyuh-luhr)

. . . .

SKEPTIC
(SKEP-tik)

. . . .

SOLICITOUS
(suh-LI-suh-tuhs)

S

unique, unusual

*Leonardo da Vinci's genius was **singular**; who else has been so talented in so many different disciplines?*

Synonyms: *exceptional, individual, odd, peculiar*

. . . .

a person who is given to skepticism, who tends to doubt or disbelieve

*When it comes to matters of faith, I tend to be a **skeptic**; I prefer to believe only when there is evidence for belief.*

Synonyms: *disbeliever, doubter*

. . . .

showing concern or care; eager

*I was irritated by their overly **solicitous** questions and fussing after my illness.*

Synonyms: *anxious, attentive, careful, worried*

SOLVENT
(SOL-vuhnt)

....

SOPORIFIC
(soh-puh-RI-fik)

....

SORDID
(SAWR-did)

(*adj.*) able to pay debts; having the power of dissolving

*After two difficult years, business was good again and at last we were **solvent**.*

stable

(*n.*) a substance, usually a liquid, in which other substances can be dissolved

*Water is a **solvent** for a variety of substances, such as salt.*

. . . .

tending to cause sleep, related to sleep or sleepiness

*While I am energized by the music of Bach, my husband finds it **soporific** and often actually falls asleep while listening to it.*

Synonyms: calming, dull, hypnotic, soothing

. . . .

characterized by baseness, filthy

*The story of his ascent to power was a **sordid** one of greed, betrayal, and even murder.*

Synonyms: degenerate, miserable, squalid, vile

SPARSE
(spahrs)

. . . .

SPECIOUS
(SPEE-shuhs)

. . . .

SPECTRUM
(SPEK-truhm)

thinly settled or grown, meager

After the long, dry summer, the grass was **sparse** *underfoot.*

Synonyms: inadequate, scanty, skimpy

. . . .

having the appearance of goodness or truth, attractive in a deceptive way

Despite her **specious** *arguments, the candidate attracted an enthusiastic following.*

Synonyms: false, illusory, misleading, plausible

. . . .

a series or range of related things or ideas

Roxanne has a wide **spectrum** *of interests, including everything from martial arts to bird watching.*

Synonyms: continuum, span

SPENDTHRIFT
(SPEND-thrift)

. . . .

SPORADIC
(spuh-RA-dik)

. . . .

SPURIOUS
(SPYOOR-ee-uhs)

a person who spends wastefully

One of my uncles is frugal and has accumulated a staggering fortune, and the other is a **spendthrift** *who has accumulated a staggering debt.*

Synonyms: spender, squanderer

. . . .

happening occasionally or irregularly

The children were given to **sporadic** *bursts of enthusiasm that their teacher was determined to cultivate.*

Synonyms: isolated, occasionally, scattered

. . . .

not genuine or true

Not wanting to hurt his feelings, she gave a **spurious** *reason for rejecting his invitation to the movies.*

Synonyms: contrived, counterfeit, deceitful, deceptive

SQUALID
(SKWO-lid)

. . . .

SQUANDER
(SKWON-duhr)

. . . .

STATIC
(STA-tik)

filthy from neglect or poverty

*Once anything makes its way into my little brother's **squalid** bedroom, it rarely makes its way out.*

Synonyms: disgusting, miserable, sordid

· ·

to spend or use wastefully, to scatter

*You worked hard to earn that money, so don't **squander** it on silly things like video games!*

Synonyms: dissipate, misuse, waste

· ·

showing a lack of change or movement

*In literature, a **static** character is one who is the same from the beginning to the end of the story.*

Synonyms: fixed, inactive, unchanging

STIGMA
(STIG-muh)

. . . .

STINT
(stint)

. . . .

STIPULATE
(STI-pyuh-leyt)

a mark or sign of disgrace

*Wendy bore the **stigma** of having been fired from three jobs, until she found a suitable career and thrived.*

Synonyms: blemish, brand, scar, stain

. . . .

a period of time spent doing a specific activity

*I had a brief **stint** in college but dropped out to start my own business.*

Synonym: term

. . . .

to set conditions of agreement, to make a specific demand

*The printer **stipulated** that the files should be ready no later than the last day of June.*

Synonyms: contract, designate, require, settle

STOIC
(STOH-ik)

. . . .

STOLID
(STO-lid)

. . . .

STRATIFIED
(STRA-tuh-fahyd)

not showing feeling

*Our mother's **stoic** attitude toward her struggle to make a living for our family was an inspiration to us.*

Synonyms: dispassionate, indifferent, philosophic, self-controlled

. . . .

having or showing no feelings

*Nobody understood what she saw in him, but she knew that his **stolid** exterior hid a sensitive soul.*

Synonyms: impassive, indifferent, unemotional

. . . .

arranged in layers or hierarchical classes

*The **stratified** cliffs of the Grand Canyon display a record of geological time.*

Synonym: ordered

STRIATED
(STRAHY-ey-ted)

. . . .

STRIDENT
(STRAHY-duhnt)

. . . .

STRUT
(struht)

marked with grooves, scratches, or stripes

*The **striated** rocks give evidence of the glaciers that once covered this region, scraping and scoring any exposed surfaces as they moved.*

Synonyms: furrowed, streaked, striped

• •

characterized by harsh and insistent sound, commanding attention

*His **strident** voice could be heard throughout the entire building.*

Synonym: loud

• •

to walk in a proud or pompous way

*Now that Henry is the boss of our division, he **struts** around as though he owns the place.*

Synonyms: flaunt, parade, swagger

STUPEFY
(STOO-puh-fahy)

. . . .

STYMIE
(STAHY-mee)

. . . .

SUBPOENA
(suh-PEE-nuh)

to make stupid or numb; to astonish

*This economics textbook is so dull that it **stupefies** more than it instructs.*

Synonyms: benumb, daze, deaden; bewilder, confound, flabbergast

. . . .

to get in the way of

*Our ambitions were **stymied** by our lack of funds.*

Synonyms: block, hinder, impede, obstruct, thwart

. . . .

a written command to appear in court

*Unless the judge issues a **subpoena**, there is no way I will appear in court.*

Synonym: summons

SUBSIDE
(suhb-SAHYD)

. . . .

SUBSTANTIATE
(suhb-STAN-shee-eyt)

. . . .

SUBTLE
(SUH-tl)

to settle down or become quiet

Before long, the storm had **subsided** *and the sun appeared.*

Synonyms: abate, diminish

. . . .

to give evidence for or prove; to give form to

It took six weeks of research for her to gather the evidence to **substantiate** *her claims, and the resulting article won several awards.*

Synonyms: demonstrate, establish; embody, materialize

. . . .

delicate or elusive, difficult to perceive or understand; insightful, skillful

The argument was so **subtle** *that I had to read the essay several times to appreciate its conclusions.*

Synonyms: indistinct, suggestive; penetrating, perceptive

SUBVERSIVE
(suhb-VUHR-siv)

. . . .

SUCCINCT
(suhk-SINGKT)

. . . .

SUCCOR
(SUH-kuhr)

GRE VOCABULARY

tending to undermine, intending to overthrow

*Because their aims were **subversive**, they distributed the pamphlets quietly, so as not to call the attention of the authorities.*

Synonyms: destructive, rebellious

. . . .

precise, using few words

*His **succinct** explanation was far more helpful than anything in our 48-page manual.*

Synonyms: blunt, concise, pithy

. . . .

relief or help; that which gives relief or help

*The missionaries vowed to give **succor** to the poor.*

Synonyms: aid, assistance

SUPERFLUOUS
(soo-PUHR-floo-uhs)

. . . .

SUPERSEDE
(soo-puhr-SEED)

. . . .

SUPPLANT
(suh-PLANT)

more than what is needed, extra, unnecessary

*Though I'm certainly grateful, your praise of my performance was **superfluous**; being able to make music is joy enough in itself.*

Synonyms: excessive, expendable, gratuitous

. . . .

to take the place or position of, displace

*In the twentieth century, the physics that followed from Einstein's theories **superseded** Newtonian physics.*

Synonyms: replace, succeed, supplant

. . . .

to take the place of, especially by force, through treachery, or through superiority

*The rebels overthrew the government, only to **supplant** one tyranny with another.*

Synonyms: overthrow, succeed, supersede, undermine, uproot

SUPPOSITION
(suh-puh-ZI-shuhn)

....

SURFEIT
(suhr-feht)

....

SYNTHESIS
(SIN-thuh-suhs)

the act of supposing or something that is supposed

Your **supposition** that I am not up to the job seems to be based more on stereotypes than on familiarity with my work.

Synonyms: assumption, hyphothesis

. . . .

an excessive amount or indulgence in something

December seems to be characterized by a **surfeit** in all things: food, drink, and gifts.

Synonyms: glut, overindulgence, satiety, surplus

. . . .

the combination of different things or ideas to form one substance or whole

The show was a remarkable **synthesis** of different art forms: drama, music, and dance combined in one extravagant spectacle.

Synonyms: amalgamation, integration, unification

TACIT
(TA-suht)

. . . .

TANGENTIAL
(tan-JENT-shuhl)

. . . .

TAUTOLOGICAL
(taw-tuh-LO-ji-kuhl)

expressed or done without words, implied

*No words on the matter were actually spoken between our neighbors and us; we simply came to a **tacit** agreement that any apples that fell onto our yard from their tree were ours.*

Synonyms: implicit, silent, suggested, unspoken

. . . .

touching or connected only slightly, as a tangent line

*Her paper was marred by the inclusion of too much information that was only **tangential** to her main point.*

Synonyms: digressive, divergent, incidental

. . . .

characterized by unnecessary repetition

*Always saying "a variety of different things" is **tautological** because the word variety already implies difference; you can simply say "a variety of things."*

Synonym: redundant

TENACITY
(tuh-NA-suh-tee)

. . . .

TENET
(TE-nuht)

. . . .

TENUOUS
(TEN-yuh-wuhs)

T

persistence

*Against all odds, with great **tenacity**, and not a little luck, she worked her way through college.*

Synonyms: determination, resolve

· ·

a principle or belief, especially one held by a particular group of people

*The main **tenet** of attachment theory is that the healthy development of a child requires the secure attachment to at least one caregiver.*

Synonyms: doctrine, precept

· ·

thin in form or density; lacking substance, strength, clarity, or a sound basis in reasoning

*We questioned her **tenuous** reasons for her three-day absence, but she refused to clarify her story.*

Synonyms: flimsy, rare; questionable, unsubstantial, vague, weak

TERSE
(tuhrs)

. . . .

TIRADE
(TAHY-reyd)

. . . .

TOME
(tohm)

concise, sometimes abruptly so

*His **terse** reply hinted at darker reasons for his condition, and so I did not press him to say more.*

Synonyms: brief, curt, pithy, succinct

• •

a long and angry speech

*Our neighbor subjects all visitors to a **tirade** on the perceived wrongdoings of his ex-wife.*

Synonyms: diatribe, harangue, invective

• •

a large, weighty, or scholarly book; one volume of a larger work

*What she originally envisioned as a brief novella developed into a 600-page **tome**, dramatizing the lives and relationships of some half-dozen characters.*

Synonym: opus

TORPOR
(TAWR-puhr)

. . . .

TORQUE
(tawrk)

. . . .

TORTUOUS
(TAWRCH-wuhs)

a state of mental and physical inactivity accompanied by a loss of feeling; a lack of energy

During my illness, the fever did not trouble me so much as the **torpor**—*I hate to be slowed down!*

Synonyms: apathy, dullness, lethargy

. . . .

a force that causes twisting or rotation, or the measurement of this force

The carpenter's drill supplied enough **torque** *to drive screws into the very dense wood.*

Synonyms: force, rotation

. . . .

having many twists or turns; characterized by indirect methods

We made our way back and forth up the **tortuous** *path through the woods.*

Synonyms: circuitous, crooked, winding; convoluted, devious

GRE VOCABULARY

TOUT
(tout)

· ·

TRACTABLE
(TRAK-tuh-buhl)

· ·

TRANSGRESSION
(tranz-GREH-shuhn)

to solicit support for, to promote

*Mr. Franklin takes every opportunity to **tout** the accomplishments of his three grandchildren.*

Synonyms: acclaim, herald, praise

. . . .

easily led, trained, or controlled; easily handled

*He has a **tractable** dog that learns tricks easily.*

Synonyms: docile, submissive, yielding; malleable

. . . .

an act of violating a command or law or of going beyond some limit

*Although our **transgression** was unintentional, we still had to pay a fine for breaking the law.*

Synonyms: breach, crime, sin, violation

TRANSIENT
(TRAN-shuhnt)

. . . .

TRANSLUCENT
(tranz-LOO-suhnt)

. . . .

TRENCHANT
(TREN-chuhnt)

passing swiftly in and out of existence, lasting
or staying only a short time

*Though they seem long, the days of summer
are **transient**, and before you know it, winter
has come again.*

Synonyms: ephemeral, fleeting, temporary,
transitory

· ·

allowing the passage of light but diffusing it so
that objects on the other side are not clearly
visible; clearly understandable; clear

***Translucent** panels were set into the wall,
so that you could see blurry figures passing
through the hallway on the other side.*

Synonyms: semitransparent; lucid

· ·

keen, articulate, or perceptive (describing
language or a person); energetic, effective;
sharply defined

*His **trenchant** criticism could be hard to take,
but the students who listened were better
writers for it.*

Synonyms: caustic, cutting; vigorous; clear-cut,
distinct

TRUCULENT
(truh-kyuh-luhnt)

. . . .

TRYST
(trist)

. . . .

feeling or showing ferocity; deadly, harsh, or aggressive

*The discipline of playing football transformed the **truculent** boy into a mild young man; he reserved his aggression for the field.*

Synonyms: brutal, cruel, fierce, savage; belligerent, hostile

. . . .

an appointment to meet, especially one made secretly between lovers

*In the myth of Pyramus and Thisbe, a **tryst** between the two lovers ends in tragedy when Pyramus believes that Thisbe has been devoured by a lioness.*

Synonyms: date, engagement, rendezvous

UBIQUITOUS
(yoo-BI-kwi-tuhs)

. . . .

UNCANNY
(uhn-KA-nee)

. . . .

UNFEIGNED
(uhn-FEYND)

existing everywhere at once

*That hit song was **ubiquitous** all summer long: I heard it at the beach, at the grocery store, waiting on line at the deli, and on the radio just about every time I turned it on.*

Synonyms: omnipresent, pervasive, widespread

. . . .

seeming to be supernatural in nature, extraordinary

*She had an **uncanny** way of knowing that someone was seriously ill, sometimes even before the person knew of the illness him or herself.*

Synonyms: eerie, mysterious, spooky, weird

. . . .

genuine, sincere

*I love to be with children, because their delight is always **unfeigned** and spontaneous.*

Synonyms: honest, real, true, unaffected

UNTENABLE
(uhn-TEN-uh-buhl)

. . . .

URBANE
(uhr-BEYN)

. . . .

incapable of being defended (describing an argument or belief); unsuitable for occupation

*The more evidence we gathered, the more clearly we saw how **untenable** our original hypothesis was, and it took us several months to devise another one.*

Synonyms: illogical, indefensible, unsound

. . . .

polite, polished, or elegant in manner

*When I was new to the city and unaccustomed to sophisticated conversation, I was thoroughly intimidated by his **urbane** wit.*

Synonyms: civilized, cultured, elegant, refined, sophisticated

GRE VOCABULARY

VACILLATE
(VA-suh-leyt)

· ·

VACUOUS
(VA-kyuh-wuhs)

· ·

VAPID
(VA-puhd)

V

to sway or fluctuate; to waver in feeling or hesitate in making a decision

*Roberta **vacillated** for so long that by the time she decided to go to the show, the tickets were all sold out.*

Synonyms: oscillate, stagger, swing; alternate, hedge, pause

. . . .

empty, lacking ideas or seriousness, idle

*I've been known on occasion to indulge in those ridiculous paperback romances—the more **vacuous**, the better.*

Synonyms: foolish, inane, purposeless, silly, stupid

. . . .

lacking energy or flavor

*The conversation at the dinner party that night was as **vapid** as the tasteless meal.*

Synonyms: dull, flat, insipid, tedious

VARIEGATED
(VER-ee-uh-gey-tuhd)

. . . .

VENERATE
(VE-nuh-reyt)

. . . .

VERACITY
(vuh-RA-suh-tee)

V

marked by a variety of colors; varied

*I love the **variegated** landscape in autumn.*

Synonyms: kaleidoscopic, motley, mottled; assorted, diverse, mixed

• •

to regard with reverence, to honor

*The basketball star was **venerated** by the citizens of the small town where he grew up.*

Synonyms: revere, worship

• •

truthfulness or accuracy

*She was a scrupulous journalist, and when she could not check the **veracity** of the claim, she struck all mentions of it from her article.*

Synonyms: authenticity, credibility, honesty

VERBOSE
(vuhr-BOHS)

. . . .

VEXATION
(vek-SEY-shuhn)

. . . .

VIABLE
(VAHY-uh-buhl)

tending to use more words than necessary, wordy

*Warren tends to write **verbose** e-mails that nobody in the company has the time to read.*

Synonyms: garrulous, long-winded, loquacious

. . . .

the act of troubling or agitating; the state of being troubled or agitated

*To be alive is to experience **vexation**; you will be happier if you accept that you will encounter annoyances.*

Synonyms: annoyance, irritation, nuisance

. . . .

capable of living, growing, and developing; able to function properly

*Though the idea was brilliant, it also involved a greater expense than was **viable**, given our budget at the time.*

Synonyms: functioning; feasible, possible, practicable, reasonable, workable

VIGILANT
(VI-juh-luhnt)

. . . .

VILIFY
(VI-luh-fahy)

. . . .

VIRTUOSO
(vir-choo-OH-soh)

V

alert, watchful

*Tourists must be **vigilant** when walking through that part of town, as the locals there tend to be especially hostile toward foreigners.*

Synonyms: attentive, guarded, wary

. . . .

to slander

*How dare you **vilify** my name in the newspaper when you are the one who has been squandering city funds.*

Synonyms: attack, censure, defame, denigrate, disparage

. . . .

(n.) one who excels at an art

*Picasso was a **virtuoso** who continuously explored different styles, materials, and themes.*

Synonyms: genius, master, prodigy

(adj.) displaying excellence

*The audience erupted in applause for the pianist's **virtuoso** performance of the Liszt étude.*

Synonyms: masterful, skilled

VIRULENT
(VIR-uh-lunt)

. . . .

VISCOUS
(VIS-kuhs)

. . . .

VITUPERATIVE
(vi-TOO-puh-ruh-tiv)

poisonous, highly infective, or deadly;
malicious or harsh

*The 1918 influenza virus was especially **virulent**,
resulting in a pandemic that killed some 50 million
people.*

Synonyms: destructive, noxious; hostile, spiteful

• •

adhesive, sticky, thick (describing a liquid)

*This varnish is **viscous** when applied and dries
to a hard gloss in just a few hours.*

Synonyms: gelatinous, gummy

• •

characterized by harsh or abusive language

*The **vituperative** editorial put the mayor on
the defensive.*

Synonyms: abusive, derisive, scolding

VOGUE
(vohg)

. . . .

VOLATILE
(VO-luh-tl)

. . . .

VORACIOUS
(vaw-REY-shuhs)

V

something that is in fashion, currently popular, or favored

*If there was ever a time when Mrs. Henderson's hairstyle was in **vogue**, it was long before any of us was born.*

Synonyms: fashion, mode, popularity

. . . .

evaporating easily; explosive, changeable

*Fearing the substitute teacher's **volatile** temper, the children were quiet and obedient.*

Synonyms: gaseous; capricious, unstable

. . . .

having a large appetite, insatiable

*The film festival briefly satisfied their **voracious** appetite for new movies.*

Synonyms: avid, gluttonous, ravenous

WARRANTED
(WAW-ruhn-tuhd)

· ·

WARY
(WER-ee)

· ·

WAVER
(WEY-vuhr)

justified

Your angry outburst at the child was simply not **warranted**; *he is only two years old and simply does not know any better.*

Synonyms: authorized, sanctioned

. . . .

cautious, watchful, on guard

Our cat is **wary** *of visitors, often hiding when they first arrive.*

Synonyms: attentive, vigilant

. . . .

to sway back and forth; to become unsteady, shake, or tremble; to vacillate in making a decision or in opinion

In the twenty-first mile of the marathon, she **wavered** *in her determination to complete the race, but the spectators cheered her on.*

Synonyms: flutter, wobble; alternate, fluctuate

WELTER
(WEL-tuhr)

. . . .

WHIMSICAL
(HWIM-zi-kuhl)

. . . .

ZEALOUS
(ZE-luhs)

(*v.*) to roll or toss, as in waves; to wallow or become immersed or involved

*The children **weltered** about in the piles of fallen leaves.*

Synonyms: heave, tumble

(*n.*) a state of disorder, a jumble

*The check was lost in the **welter** of books and papers that cluttered her desk.*

Synonyms: confusion, tormoil

. . . .

full of whims, characterized by sudden and eccentric ideas

*She designs fabrics with **whimsical** patterns that are suitable for children's clothing.*

Synonyms: fanciful, playful, wayward

. . . .

characterized by passionate loyalty and zeal for a person or idea

*A **zealous** fan of the handsome young rock star, she traveled from city to city to see him perform.*

Synonyms: ardent, dedicated, devoted, impassioned